IMMIGRATION NATION

THE AMERICAN
IDENTITY
IN THE
TWENTY-FIRST
CENTURY

Judy Dodge Cummings

Illustrated by Richard Chapman

Nomad Press
A division of Nomad Communications
10 9 8 7 6 5 4 3 2 1

This book was manufactured by Versa Press,
East Peoria, Illinois
April 2019, Job #J18-13157

ISBN Softcover: 978-1-61930-763-6
ISBN Hardcover: 978-1-61930-760-5

Educational Consultant, Marla Conn

Questions regarding the ordering of this book should be addressed to
Nomad Press
2456 Christian St.
White River Junction, VT 05001
www.nomadpress.net

Titles in the Inquire & Investigate
Social Issues of the Twentieth Century set

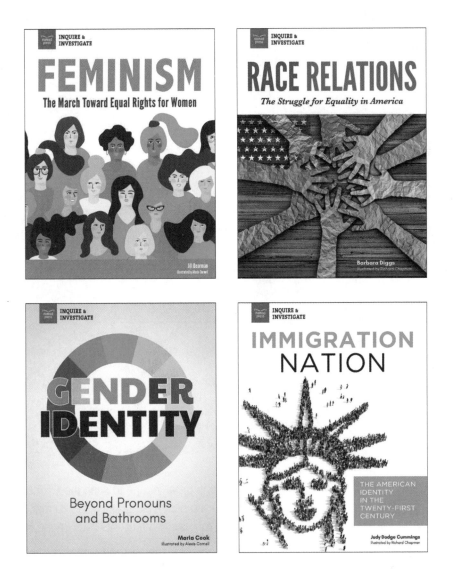

You can use a smartphone or tablet app to scan the QR codes and explore more! Cover up neighboring QR codes to make sure you're scanning the right one. You can find a list of URLs on the Resources page.

If the QR code doesn't work, try searching the internet with the Keyword Prompts to find other helpful sources.

🔍 Immigration

Interested in primary sources? Look for this icon.

What are source notes?

In this book, you'll find small numbers at the end of some paragraphs. These numbers indicate that you can find source notes for that section in the back of the book. Source notes tell readers where the writer got their information. This might be a news article, a book, or another kind of media. Source notes are a way to know that what you are reading is information that other people have verified. They can also lead you to more places where you can explore a topic that you're curious about!

Contents

TIMELINE

1607.......................... The first permanent colony of immigrants from England settles in Jamestown, Virginia.

1798.......................... The U.S. Congress passes the Alien and Sedition Acts, increasing residency requirements to obtain citizenship and giving the president broad powers to deport immigrants.

1840–1860................. A first wave of immigrants surges into the United States from northern and western Europe.

1870–1920................. A second wave of immigrants enters the United States from southern and eastern Europe.

1882.......................... Congress passes the Chinese Exclusion Act, barring most Chinese from immigrating to the United States.

1892.......................... The immigrant processing center on Ellis Island in New York Harbor opens.

1910.......................... The Angel Island processing center in San Francisco Bay opens.

1921 and 1924.......... Congress passes two laws establishing a national-origin quota system to limit the entry of immigrants from certain areas of the world.

1942–1964................. The Bracero Program brings thousands of Mexican laborers to the United States to work in agriculture.

1965.......................... Congress passes the Immigration and Nationality Act, ending the national-origin quota system and focusing on family reunification.

2001.......................... The DREAM Act is first introduced in Congress.

2006.......................... Massive protests against a hardline immigration bill create a political divide between Democrats and Republicans.

June 15, 2012............ President Barack Obama signs an executive order creating the Deferred Action on Childhood Arrivals (DACA) program.

2013.......................... For the first year in American history, the majority of newborn babies are not white.

January 27, 2017....... President Donald Trump signs an executive order that immediately bans immigrants from seven primarily Muslim countries, creating chaos in American airports.

September 5, 2017..... The Trump administration announces it is phasing out the DACA program.

May 7, 2018............... U.S. Attorney General Jeff Sessions announces the administration's zero-tolerance immigrant enforcement, which includes separating parents and children apprehended at the U.S. border.

June 20, 2018............ President Trump signs an executive order ending the policy of separating families apprehended at the border.

2045.......................... The year demographers predict that non-Hispanic whites will no longer make up the majority of people living in the United States.

PROCESS OF LEGAL IMMIGRATION

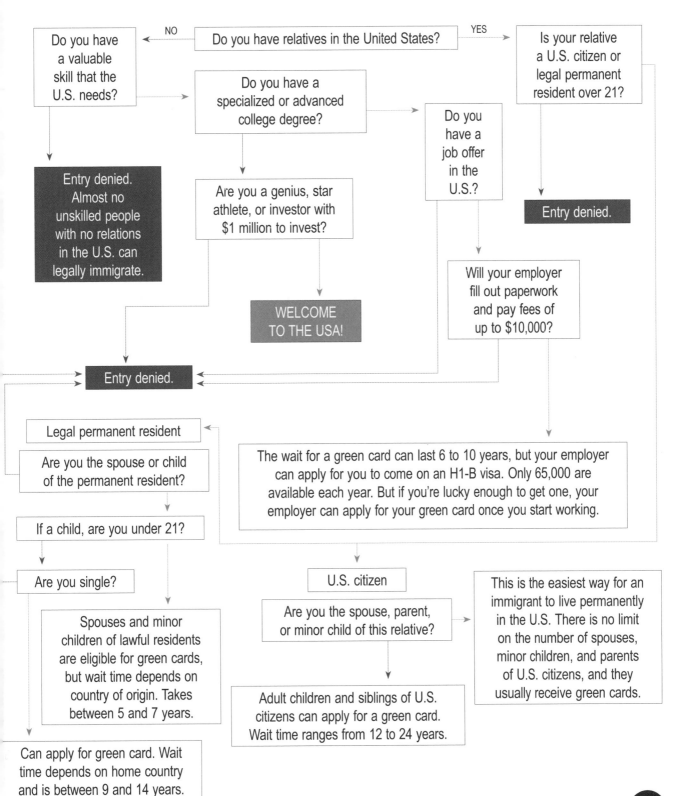

Do you have relatives in the United States?

NO → Do you have a valuable skill that the U.S. needs?

YES → Is your relative a U.S. citizen or legal permanent resident over 21?

Do you have a specialized or advanced college degree?

Do you have a job offer in the U.S.?

Entry denied. Almost no unskilled people with no relations in the U.S. can legally immigrate.

Are you a genius, star athlete, or investor with $1 million to invest?

Entry denied.

WELCOME TO THE USA!

Will your employer fill out paperwork and pay fees of up to $10,000?

Entry denied.

Legal permanent resident

Are you the spouse or child of the permanent resident?

The wait for a green card can last 6 to 10 years, but your employer can apply for you to come on an H1-B visa. Only 65,000 are available each year. But if you're lucky enough to get one, your employer can apply for your green card once you start working.

If a child, are you under 21?

Are you single?

Spouses and minor children of lawful residents are eligible for green cards, but wait time depends on country of origin. Takes between 5 and 7 years.

U.S. citizen

Are you the spouse, parent, or minor child of this relative?

This is the easiest way for an immigrant to live permanently in the U.S. There is no limit on the number of spouses, minor children, and parents of U.S. citizens, and they usually receive green cards.

Adult children and siblings of U.S. citizens can apply for a green card. Wait time ranges from 12 to 24 years.

Can apply for green card. Wait time depends on home country and is between 9 and 14 years.

Introduction ▶ The Golden Door

What does it mean to be an immigrant today?

Whether a person is fleeing for their life or seeking new opportunities, an immigrant is looking toward a new nation for security, hope, and potential. How should the government and citizens of that new nation react to immigrants? That question is at the heart of much debate in the twenty-first century.

For more than a century, an immigrant from France has stood vigil in New York Harbor. Standing 350 feet tall, this lady is hard to miss. Dressed in a robe of green copper, she wears a spiked crown. With a tablet of laws clutched in one hand and a torch held aloft in the other, the Statue of Liberty cries out to the world:

> "Give me your tired, your poor, your huddled masses yearning to breathe free . . . .
> I lift my lamp beside the golden door!"

Millions of immigrants have answered Lady Liberty's call, passing over, under, and through the "Golden Door" to become Americans. But today, in the early twenty-first century, the people of the United States are questioning these words of welcome that are mounted on a bronze plaque in the Statue of Liberty Museum. On the eve of its 250th birthday, the United States finds itself in the middle of an identity crisis as it grapples with major decisions about immigration.

IMMIGRATION DEBATE

Should this land of immigrants allow other foreign-born individuals to move here, people desperate for freedom and hungry for opportunity? Or should the United States shut the Golden Door, barring entry to all but a select few?

America's struggle is nothing new. Although the nation celebrates its immigrant past in song and story, throughout history the United States has struggled with this complicated question: What does it mean to be an American?

The Statue of Liberty in New York City

credit: Don Ramey Logan (CC BY 4.0)

The way citizens and political leaders answer this question determines who can enter the country, who can stay in the country, and who can become citizens of the country. The answer to this question will determine the future of American identity in the twenty-first century.

The United States has always been a nation of immigrants, and today is no exception. Walk down the streets of New York City and you can hear conversations in English, Spanish, Urdu, and Korean. Go out to dinner in Minneapolis, Minnesota, and you can feast on cachapas from Colombia, okra stew from Liberia, or beef tagine from Morocco. Attend a soccer game in rural Wisconsin and you can cheer on the European-American kid who kicks the ball to the Mexican-American kid who passes it to the Hmong-American kid who scores a goal. Immigrants are everywhere, from the halls of the U.S. Congress to the teacher at the front of your classroom. Perhaps you see an immigrant when you look in the mirror.

You can hear examples of some of the languages immigrants speak in New York City at this website. What concerns do these immigrants have about their languages? What role does language have in shaping a person's identity?

Here and Now immigrant languages

A protest march in support of immigration, 2017

credit: Social Justice - Bruce Emmerling (CC BY 1.0)

To understand the debate in the United States over immigration, you must first understand how the process works. In this book, immigrants will help explain the experience of giving up their homelands in the hopes of a new and better life in America. All their stories are true.

IMMIGRATION PROCESS

Meet Javier, the first of several immigrants you will meet in this book. Javier (a pseudonym) was born in Mexico City, Mexico, in 1981. A child of divorced parents, he had no contact with his father and lived with his little brother and mother. When Javier was 12 years old, his mother fell in love with a man from the United States and they decided to marry. When his mother told Javier they were going to emigrate and leave Mexico forever, the boy had mixed feelings. Javier's grandparents and cousins lived in Mexico. Love for family made him want to stay.

> Still, the thought of moving to the United States sounded like a "great adventure."

In the summer of 1995, the American man obtained special visas for his fiancée and her children. Javier, along with his mother and brother, flew to Colorado, the home of his soon-to-be stepfather. Now, Javier was an immigrant, because he had entered another country with plans to stay permanently.

The family drove to El Paso, Texas, for an interview with immigration officials. They asked Javier's mother many questions. Was she educated? Did she have any money in the bank? Had she committed any crimes? Her fiancé had to show evidence that he could support her and her children so they would not become a burden to the U.S. government.

PRIMARY SOURCES

Primary sources come from people who were eyewitnesses to events. They might write about the event, take pictures, post short messages to social media or blogs, or record the event for radio or video. The photographs in this book are primary sources, taken at the time of the event. Paintings of events are usually not primary sources, since they are often painted long after the event took place. What other primary sources can you find? Why are primary sources important? Do you learn differently from primary sources than from secondary sources, which come from people who did not directly experience the event?

PS

Immigrants have made significant contributions throughout the history of the United States. Check out this website to see who the editors of *Buzzworthy* identified as immigrants worthy of hall-of-fame status. What criteria would you use to select immigrants who belong in a hall of fame as great Americans?

🔍 Buzzworthy famous immigrants

IDENTITY NEWS

Throughout history, people have migrated from one region to another, crossing oceans and continents. But in the modern age, no one is allowed to cross international borders without permission from the government of the country they want to enter.

The family passed the interview. Javier's mother and the American were wed, and Javier's life in the United States began. As you will read later, sometimes the boy did indeed find his new life "thrilling," but, all too often in those first few years, life as an immigrant was confusing and lonely.

Think of immigration law as a security system for the United States' metaphorical Golden Door. Only certain immigrants have the key to unlock that door.

Javier's mother had the code. Because her fiancé was an American citizen who sponsored her and because she had savings and an education, the U.S. government granted her the status of lawful permanent resident, more commonly known as an immigrant with a green card. A person with a green card permit has many rights and freedoms, but still must meet certain conditions in order to remain in the United States.

There are other ways to immigrate, too. Let's meet some immigrants lined up outside the Golden Door.

The first immigrant is a billionaire. He plans to invest a lot of money in a company that will create jobs in the United States. That investment unlocks the Golden Door and he enters.

The next immigrant has invented a high-tech gadget with great potential. The United States wants her skills. Buzz—the Golden Door unlocks and swings open.

A large group of immigrants enters next. These people do not have advanced skills, but they are willing to pick crops during harvest season and wait on tables during the tourist season. The United States needs their labor, so the Golden Door opens. Known as guest workers, these immigrants do not get to remain in the country permanently. Once the season ends, they must go home.

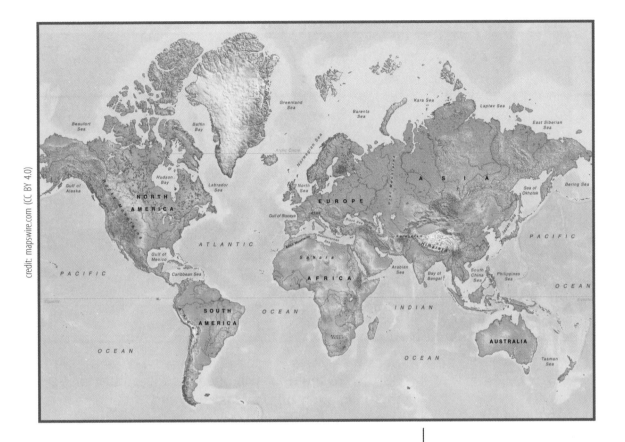

The next immigrant gambles and wins. He comes from an area of the world that doesn't tend to send many immigrants to the United States. That allows him to enter his name in the diversity lottery. Only a limited number of names are drawn each year, so this man is lucky. His name is selected and he passes through the Golden Door.

The last group of immigrants looks weary, as though they have traveled far and seen much. They are refugees. They fled their country because they fear government persecution, violence, or even death. You might think the Golden Door would open automatically for them. Aren't these the very sort of people Lady Liberty is referring to when she says, "Give me your tired, your poor, your huddled masses yearning to breathe free?"

VOCAB LAB

There is a lot of new vocabulary in this book! Turn to the glossary in the back when you come to a word you don't understand. Practice your new vocabulary in the VOCAB LAB activities in each chapter.

The Rio Grande City Border Patrol agents apprehend 102 undocumented immigrants, 2016.

credit: U.S. Customs and Border Protection

In the middle of the immigration debate stand the immigrants—both legal residents and those without proper documentation. As the nation argues, these individuals work to build a new life, unsure of what the future holds.

But before the door will open, refugees must prove to immigration officials that they are in genuine danger in their home countries. If they can't prove it, the door stays shut. Each year, the president and Congress set a cap on how many refugees may enter the country. In 2017, the cap was 50,000, and that limit was reached by July that year.[1]

According to the law, the Golden Door should close after 675,000 permanent residency cards have been granted for the year. However, the number of immigrants that enter the United States exceeds that number every year.

The immigration cap is exceeded each year for two reasons. For one thing, since 1965, the goal of the U.S. immigration system has been family reunification. Therefore, close family members who immigrate are not counted in the annual cap. The second reason the United States exceeds its annual cap is because many immigrants do not enter the country through the Golden Door.

These people do not have a close family member in the United States to legally sponsor them, millions of dollars to invest in the U.S. economy, or a highly valued skill. Plus, they cannot prove they are refugees. These individuals enter and remain in the United States without receiving permission to stay long-term, even if that is their intention.

The tens of thousands of people who live in the United States without legal permission are called undocumented immigrants.

IMMIGRATION NATION

Census data from 2016 reveals that 43.7 million foreign-born people live in the United States. Roughly half of these people are naturalized citizens. The other half are divided as follows: 13.1 million are lawful permanent residents; 11.1 million are undocumented immigrants: and 1.7 million hold temporary visas.[2] These foreign-born compose approximately 13.5 percent of the U.S. population, the highest percentage in more than a century.[3]

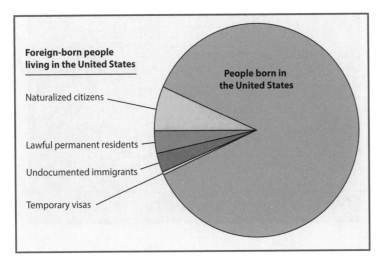

Foreign-born people living in the United States

People born in the United States

Naturalized citizens

Lawful permanent residents

Undocumented immigrants

Temporary visas

The United States is not the only nation to which immigrants flock. Immigration is a global phenomenon. According to the United Nations, in 2000, there were 173 million international immigrants (2.8 percent of the world's population). By 2015, the total number of immigrants around the world had increased to 244 million people, which was 3.3 percent of the global population. Slightly more than half of international immigrants are male; and most people migrate when they are between the ages of 25 and 50.

Immigrants come from India and China, from Mexico and the Philippines, from Honduras and Vietnam, and countless other places. They come for opportunity and security, to reunite with family, or to pursue the American dream. They come through legal channels and live out in the open, and they come through back channels and live in the shadows. Some immigrants are welcomed, others are shunned. Some become citizens, while others are deported.

The United States immigration system has not been overhauled since 1965 and is long overdue for change. Lawmakers agree that the system is flawed, but they do not agree on how to fix it. Ultimately, the authority to change immigration law belongs to Congress, but year after year, Republicans and Democrats fail to reach a compromise.

In the face of Congress's inaction, other branches of government have taken steps to fix the immigration system.

Bronze plaque inside the Statue of Liberty

credit: StatueLibrtyNPS (CC BY 2.0)

Presidents have used executive power to favor or ban certain groups of immigrants. State legislators have passed laws that require local police to investigate people they suspect to be undocumented immigrants. Some mayors have declared their cities sanctuaries and forbid local police departments from helping federal agents. Citizens have risen up to support or oppose the actions of their political leaders, facing off across a chasm that is deep and wide.

In the following pages, you will read a collection of stories from the perspectives of lawmakers, U.S. Border Patrol agents, activists, and the immigrants themselves. You will also encounter facts—statistics, laws, and court decisions. Consider the perspectives and the facts together. Stories without facts are just opinion, and facts without stories erase the human face of immigration.

This book puts you in the role of investigator. You will explore the long history of America's immigrant past and assess the role of the law as gatekeeper. You will examine who immigrates, how and why they come, and how they are treated. As you engage in the activities and consider the facts and stories, keep in mind these tough questions. What does it mean to be an American in the twenty-first century? Does Lady Liberty's welcome still hold true or is it time to change the words on her bronze plaque? Should the United States open or close its Golden Door?

VOCAB LAB 📖

Write down what you think each word means. What root words can you find to help you? What does the context of the word tell you?

green card, **diversity lottery**, **immigrant**, **prejudice**, **refugee**, and **undocumented immigrant**.

Compare your definitions with those of your friends or classmates. Did you all come up with the same meanings? Turn to the text and glossary if you need help.

KEY QUESTIONS

- **Do you have any personal experience with immigration? How does this experience influence your views?**
- **What do you hope to learn about immigration?**

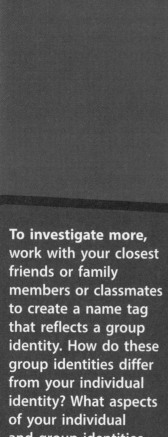

HELLO, MY NAME IS . . .

As you investigate immigration and the American identity in the twenty-first century, keep a journal to record your thoughts and discoveries. Begin your immigration journal with an exploration of your own identity. Who are you? What is your name? What aspects of your identity are not revealed by your name? In this activity, you are going to design a name tag that reflects who you are as a whole person.

- **Develop a list of questions to ask yourself in order to clarify what you believe and how you see your place in the world.** Consider the origins of your given name or nickname, hobbies and interests, your place in your family, physical characteristics, and background, including race, religion, ethnicity, and place of birth.

- **What images, words, and materials help define your identity questions?** Consider using quotes from people or books, words that describe your inner and outer self, images or illustrations of things you value, or materials that symbolize something you enjoy.

- **Make a prediction.** When family, friends, or classmates see your name tag, will they be able to understand how you define yourself?

- **Test your prediction.** Introduce yourself to some of your peers by showing them your name tag and asking, "Who am I?" How do they respond? Is their understanding of your identity significantly different from how you view yourself? What could you change about your name tag to give others a better understanding of who you are?

To investigate more, work with your closest friends or family members or classmates to create a name tag that reflects a group identity. How do these group identities differ from your individual identity? What aspects of your individual and group identities remain the same?

Chapter 1
A Backward Look

IT'S INTERESTING THAT THERE ARE SO MANY DIFFERENT TYPES OF IMMIGRANTS...

How has immigration changed from the early days of the American colonies to today?

The laws and attitudes surrounding immigration have always been complicated, despite the fact that, except for Native Americans, everyone living in the United States is an immigrant or of immigrant descent.

The United States has a love-hate relationship with immigrants. On St. Patrick's Day, people with only a hint of Irish ancestry proudly wear green. On Cinco de Mayo, restaurants do a brisk business selling tacos to people with no Mexican heritage. The United States proudly presents itself as a nation built by immigrants who achieved the American dream.

But this rosy picture does not tell the whole story. All of us living in the United States today—except Native Americans—have immigrant ancestors perched in our family tree. At key moments throughout American history, waves of immigrants poured through the Golden Door. Although some were welcomed for the land they settled and the labor they performed, each wave also met a tide of xenophobia determined to push it back to sea.

To understand immigration today, we must first look backward to America's past.

COLONIAL AMERICA

Students in elementary school learn about the first European immigrants to North America. John Smith (1580–1631) arrived in Virginia in 1607 and met the Powhatan princess Pocahontas (c. 1596–1617). Pilgrims came on the *Mayflower* to Massachusetts and celebrated the first Thanksgiving with their Wampanoag neighbors in 1621. By the 1630s, immigration to colonial America was so common that the details of each arrival went unrecorded. Some statistics tell the story of these early immigrants.

Between 1630 and 1700, approximately 172,000 immigrants settled the East Coast.

Most who fled England did so to pray in peace. New England, New Jersey, Pennsylvania, and Maryland were colonies founded by Christian minorities who faced persecution in England. Between 1713 and 1765, another 210,000 Europeans joined the earlier settlers, half from Ireland and the rest from Germany, Holland, and Scotland.[1]

THE FIRST BACKLASH

The end of the Revolutionary War in 1783 triggered a new wave of European emigration. At first, the United States welcomed these newcomers, who could become naturalized citizens after only five years. Then, in 1798, immigrants suddenly became "the enemy." Why?

In 1794, President George Washington (1732–1799) had signed a treaty with Britain. France was at war with Britain at the time, and Washington's move enraged the French government. By 1798, the United States and France were on the brink of war.

Look at the timeline of immigration to America from 1607 to 2016. What are three factors that brought immigrants to the United States during these 400 years?

timeline history American immigration

COMING IN CHAINS

Africans came to America during the colonial era, but they came in chains, not by choice. In 1619, a Dutch vessel docked in Jamestown, Virginia, with 20 captive Africans in its cargo hold. This was the birth of American slavery. The international slave trade lasted until the late 1860s. During this time, slave merchants kidnapped 12 million Africans and transported them across the Atlantic. Half a million of these captives were taken to North America.

In 2015, the Broadway musical *Hamilton* took the nation by storm. The song "Immigrants: We Get the Job Done" by Lin-Manuel Miranda (1980–) highlighted the role of immigrants. What is the message of this song?

YouTube We Get Job Done

IDENTITY NEWS

Why is freedom of speech a crucial element of democracy?

Two rival political parties fanned the flames of xenophobia. Federalists supported close ties with Britain, while Democratic-Republicans wanted to ally with France. As tensions between the United States and France grew, Federalists whipped the public into a panic about the 25,000 French immigrants in America, suggesting they might be spies plotting to overthrow American democracy. What Federalists who controlled the White House and Congress really feared was a loss of political power.

In the summer of 1798, Congress passed the Alien and Sedition Acts. These laws increased residency requirements for U.S. citizenship from five years to 14 and authorized President Adams to deport immigrants deemed dangerous. Most controversially, the laws banned "false, scandalous, and malicious writing" against Congress or the president. Journalists were not allowed to write articles that criticized lawmakers. The ink had barely dried on the Bill of Rights when freedom of speech and of the press were being violated.

Tensions between France and the United States faded, and, in 1801, the Alien and Sedition Acts expired. However, this was not the last time immigrants were labeled the enemy.

A political cartoon from 1798 showing a Federalist and Democratic-Republican duking it out with fire tongs

FIRST WAVE

In the middle of the nineteenth century, a torrent of immigrants flowed into the United States. From 170,000 people arriving each year in the 1840s, the number surged to 260,000 a year by the 1850s. Historians call this surge the "first wave of immigration."

Seven out of every 10 newcomers came from Ireland or Germany. Starvation was what pushed the Irish from home. When the potato blight destroyed one-third of Ireland's potato crop in 1845, people suffered horribly. Ireland's population shrank as 1 million people died and another million emigrated to America.

Many Germans emigrated to escape persecution, while others came for land. In 1848, a political movement swept Germany. Its leaders demanded democracy and human rights. When this revolution failed, activists fled to the United States to escape arrest. Plus, the United States still had plenty of cheap land, and in the 1850s, a million Germans settled Midwestern states to farm.

The first wave also brought Chinese immigrants to California.

Many Chinese immigrants became fisherman, including these two Chinese shrimp fishers in San Francisco Bay, c. 1888.

credit: Gulf of Maine Cod Project, NOAA National Marine Sanctuaries; Courtesy of National Archives

On April 21, 1847, Hannah Curtis wrote to her brother, who had emigrated. What hardships does Hannah mention? What does she ask her brother for?

🔍 Hannah Curtis letter

This image of an Irish woman named Bridget O'Donnell, who suffered during the famine, appeared in an English newspaper in 1849.

credit: Illustrated London News, December 22, 1849

In China, land was scarce, taxes were high, and the government oppressed citizens. Dreams of striking it rich with gold lured Chinese immigrants to what they called "Gold Mountain." They worked in mining and railroads and opened small businesses.

FIRST-WAVE BACKLASH

Religion, language, and race set immigrants of the first wave apart from earlier newcomers. While most settlers in the colonial era were Protestant, the Irish were Roman Catholic, the Germans were either Catholic or Jewish, and the Chinese were Buddhist. While many Irish spoke English, the Germans and Chinese did not. Plus, the Chinese were Asian, not white. Native-born Americans (not to be confused with Native Americans) viewed these differences with fear.

Nativist newspapers described the Irish and Germans as corrupt, lazy, and drunkards. People feared Catholic immigrants would be more devoted to the pope than the president. And because immigrants were willing to work for low pay, native-born workers accused immigrants of stealing their jobs and driving down wages.

In the 1850s, Nativists formed the Know-Nothing political party. Its platform was anti-immigrant. The Know-Nothing Party was short-lived. In 1856, it broke up because of disagreements about the issue of slavery, and gradually Irish and German immigrants assimilated into society.

This was not true, however, for Chinese immigrants on the Pacific coast. When that region's economy slumped, racial tensions flared. Native-born Americans resented Chinese immigrants, who competed for scare jobs.

IDENTITY NEWS

The platform of the Know-Nothing Party called for restrictions on immigration, a ban on voting or holding office for people born outside the United States, and a 21-year residency requirement for becoming a citizen.

In 1882, Congress passed the Chinese Exclusion Act, which banned Chinese contract laborers from immigrating and labeled all Chinese as "aliens ineligible for citizenship."

SECOND WAVE

Ellis Island, New York

Between 1870 and 1920, a second wave brought more than 26 million immigrants onto America's shores. Most of these people came from southern and eastern Europe in steamships across the Atlantic Ocean. Vessels docked in New York Harbor, where, in 1892, the federal government opened a processing center on Ellis Island. Here, foreigners went through a legal and medical inspection to enter the country.

Because the United States needed immigrant labor for its mines and factories, government officials admitted 98 percent of the people who came through Ellis Island. This was not true for those who arrived on the West Coast. The Chinese Exclusion Act barred Chinese laborers from immigrating.

Angel Island, San Francisco, California

retrieved from: Library of Congress

IDENTITY NEWS

Some second-wave
immigrants were socialists,
with political views that
alarmed lawmakers.

Chinese tourists, merchants, and students could still enter the United States, however. In 1910, a station was opened on Angel Island in the San Francisco Bay to process immigrants from Asia. Many immigrants were detained on Angel Island, some as long as two years.

SECOND-WAVE BACKLASH

When the second wave began in 1870, immigration to the United States was unrestricted. Fifty years later, the wave ended when the federal government enacted the tightest immigration laws in history.

At the turn of the twentieth century, the United States was a country in transition. In 1880, only one in seven people lived in a city. Then, the Industrial Revolution transformed the economy. The invention of electricity led to businessmen building factories and hiring immigrants to work their assembly lines. Urban populations grew rapidly, and city governments suddenly faced the problems of pollution, crime, slums, and political corruption.

Second-wave immigrants were mostly uneducated and unskilled. Some looked different from first-wave immigrants. Many were Jewish or Eastern Orthodox Christian, religions unfamiliar to Americans.

Americans blamed the newcomers for the overcrowded, crime-infested cities, so politicians acted. Between 1891 and 1917, a series of laws blocked immigrants from entering the United States for reasons ranging from contagious disease to moral defects.

Congress passed quotas that
targeted specific ethnic groups.

The Emergency Immigration Act of 1921 restricted the number of new immigrants per year to 3 percent of the number of residents from each country who were living in the United States according to the 1910 census. Two years later, the quota for each nation dropped to 2 percent of each country's foreign-born population in the United States, based on the 1890 census.

In 1890, most of the foreign-born in the United States came from northwestern Europe, so this "national-origin" system was designed to exclude immigrants from southern and eastern Europe and from continents other than Europe. The quota system was so effective at excluding these immigrants that, by 1960, seven out of every 10 immigrants to the United States were European, most from Western Europe.

FAMILY REUNIFICATION

During the 1960s, the Civil Rights Movement launched the United States into a new era. African Americans pushed for equality in education, employment, and voting. Lawmakers decided it was time to eliminate prejudice in immigration law, too.

On October 3, 1965, the Statute of Liberty watched as President Lyndon Johnson (1908–1973) signed the Immigration and Nationality Act. "This new law," Johnson said, "corrects a cruel and enduring wrong in the conduct of the American nation." National quotas were abandoned, and the Golden Door opened to immigrants from around the world.

Critics opposed this change, dreading a deluge of poor Africans, Asians, and Latin Americans. So, conservative lawmakers changed the law in a way they believed would keep immigrants white and European.

DO NOT ENTER

Laws passed during the late nineteenth and early twentieth centuries excluded immigrants who fit these categories.

- Contagious disease
- Polygamist
- Felon
- Contract laborer
- Physical or mental defect
- Unaccompanied children
- Anarchist
- Illiterate
- Feebleminded
- Women coming for immoral purposes

A 1921 political cartoon shows the government response to the influx of immigrants.

retrieved from: Library of Congress

The original bill favored immigrants with skills the United States needed. Opponents insisted this be changed to give priority to immigrants with family members already living in the country. The final version of the law gave family members of U.S. citizens and lawful permanent residents 80 percent of the available visas. People with specialized skills received only 20 percent. The law capped annual immigration at 290,000, but spouses, minor children, and parents of U.S. citizens were not included in this limit.

Ironically, the family reunification focus had the opposite effect of what opponents wanted. Under the new law, if even a few Asian, African, and Latin American immigrants became legal residents, they could sponsor close family members to immigrate. Those family members could sponsor their relatives, and so on and so on.

The Immigration and Nationality Act caused a huge shift in U.S. demographics. In 1960, 75 percent of the foreign-born population in the United States came from Europe. By 2015, Europeans composed only 11.1 percent of immigrants. The 1965 law opened the Golden Door to the world at a time when few Western Europeans wanted to emigrate. During the 1960s, their homelands were secure and stable.

People from Mexico, China, India, the Philippines, El Salvador, Vietnam, Cuba, the Dominican Republic, South Korea, and beyond, however, were eager for opportunity or desperate for freedom. In the last third of the twentieth century, they came in a third great wave. Every decade since 1965, legal immigration has added another 11 million people to the United States, mostly from Latin America and Asia.[2]

President Johnson speaking by the Statue of Liberty in 1965

credit: Yoichi Okamoto

Congress has tweaked the law a few times to try to slow the pace of immigration, but these tweaks have not worked. Not everyone has immigrated legally.

UNDOCUMENTED IMMIGRATION

During the second wave, the federal government took control of the immigration system. Immigrants were required to apply for a visa at a U.S. embassy in their home country and present it to customs agents when they entered the United States. But what about people who, for a variety of reasons, couldn't get the legal papers they needed?

Originally, most undocumented immigrants came from Mexico. Mexicans had been entering the United States for decades. They settled in the Southwest, where seasonal agricultural work was plentiful. During World War II, the United States and Mexican governments created the Bracero Program, which brought 4.6 million Mexicans to the United States under temporary visas to work in agriculture and on the railroads. When the program ended in 1964, many Braceros remained.

> By the 1980s, the public outcry about the number of undocumented immigrants in the country grew so loud that lawmakers acted.

In 1986, the Immigration Reform and Control Act (IRCA) targeted employers who hired undocumented immigrants—businesses had to prove their workers were legal residents. Undocumented immigration continued, however, as both businesses and immigrants forged the necessary documents.

Go to the National Museum of American History website to learn about the Bracero Program. Look at the photographs and read the accompanying text. Based on this information, did the Bracero Program provide opportunity to Mexican immigrants or exploit them?

American history bittersweet

IDENTITY NEWS

IRCA granted amnesty to immigrants without papers who had lived in the United States for five years.

A Mexican woman picking cotton in Texas

credit: Hollem, Howard R., 1942

VOCAB LAB

Write down what you think each word means. What root words can you find to help you? What does the context of the word tell you?

amnesty, **census**, **demographics**, **economy**, **illiterate**, **quota**, **slum**, **tenement**, and **xenophobia**.

Compare your definitions with those of your friends or classmates. Did you all come up with the same meanings? Turn to the text and glossary if you need help.

In 1996, Congress tried again. The Illegal Immigration Reform and Immigrant Responsibility Act barred undocumented immigrants caught in the United States from applying for legal residency for three years. The government was given more power to deport legal residents convicted of serious crimes, and a wall was built between San Diego, California, and Tijuana, Mexico.

As the twentieth century ended, undocumented immigration showed no signs of stopping. People trying to immigrate legally waited years, sometimes decades. When President George W. Bush (1946–) was inaugurated in 2001, he vowed to reform the system.

Then on September 11, 2001, a group of immigrants from the Middle East launched a terrorist attack that struck at the nation's heart. The 9/11 tragedy transformed immigration into a national security issue. Lawmakers abandoned reform plans in favor of beefing up the border and deporting immigrants without permission to be in the country legally.

Immigration in the twenty-first century is greatly affected by the history of people coming to this country. In the next chapter, we'll take a look at some of the paths different immigrants have followed through the Golden Door.

KEY QUESTIONS

- **What is the relationship between attitudes toward immigrants and the economy? Why?**

- **Almost everyone in this country is a descendent of an immigrant. How should this fact inform the historical debate on immigration?**

- **Why does it matter what country immigrants come from?**

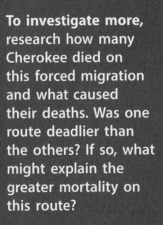
REFLECT

In 1830, Congress passed the Indian Removal Act, which authorized the federal government to move five Native American tribes to Indian Territory (today's Oklahoma). Native Americans became involuntary immigrants. In the spring of 1838, the U.S. Army forced 15,000 Cherokee off their land in Georgia and made them march hundreds of miles west on a journey known as the Trail of Tears. What routes did these immigrants follow and how long did it take them to reach their destination? What can maps tell us about the conditions people faced on this journey?

* **Use the maps on this website to locate and measure the main routes the Cherokee took west.** These include the Northern Route, the Benge Route, and the Water Route.

 NPS trail of tears map

* **What tools do you need to measure the routes?** How many miles is each route?

* **Assuming people walked eight hours a day, how many days would it take on each trail to reach Indian Territory?** Consider the average length of an adult's stride, the number of feet in a mile, average walking speed, and average steamboat speed.

* **Based on your calculations, which route was the fastest?** How would you adjust your calculations to account for people who traveled by ox-drawn wagon, the pace of children and the elderly, or steep terrain?

> **To investigate more,** research how many Cherokee died on this forced migration and what caused their deaths. Was one route deadlier than the others? If so, what might explain the greater mortality on this route?

GRAPH THE NUMBERS

Sometimes visual aids such as graphs are helpful when thinking about lots of complex information. Design a series of graphs to communicate the history of U.S. immigration. Locate data at the Digital Scholarship Lab's interactive website.

🔍 Digital scholarship Lab

- **What changes in immigration do you want to show?** Consider the following factors.

  - The rise and fall in the total number of immigrants from 1850 to 2010

  - The most common countries of origin of immigrants in 1850, 1950, and 2010

  - The percentage of the U.S. population that was foreign-born at different times in history

- **What types of graphs most effectively illustrate these changes—a pie chart, bar graph, or line graph?** Create a series of graphs and have a classmate try to read them. Are they successful?

> **To investigate more,** choose one 50-year period between 1820 and 2010 and research the major world events that occurred then. What is the connection between these events and the trends in immigration at that time? How could you display these findings on a graph?

Chapter 2
The Gatekeepers

THE FIRST STEP TOWARD CITIZENSHIP IS LAWFUL PERMANENT RESIDENCY.

Why do we need laws to govern and oversee immigration?

United States immigration law is complicated and confusing, but it's necessary to have a structure in place so people will be treated as fairly and as efficiently as possible. However, many people believe immigration law desperately needs an upgrade.

The Golden Door is regulated by immigration law, which acts as a kind of security system. Only certain people have the code to disarm this system and enter the country. Anyone who tries to sneak in risks being detained by the agencies that enforce the law—Immigration and Customs Enforcement (ICE), Customs and Border Protection (CBP), and United States Citizenship and Immigration Service (USCIS).

Immigration law has three main goals: reunify families, recruit skilled workers, and protect refugees. Sounds simple, right?

Wrong! United States immigration law is complicated and confusing. There are dozens of visa categories —a fashion model does not apply for the same visa as an athlete. The sister of an American citizen is judged differently from the parent of a legal resident. The immigrants who can afford a lawyer to steer them through the process are the lucky ones. Let's explore some ways immigrants enter the Golden Door.

FAMILY REUNIFICATION

The easiest way for immigrants to get permanent residency is for a relative who is a U.S. citizen or lawful permanent resident to sponsor them. That was Procopio's story.

Born in Mexico City, Procopio had a stable job with the Mexican government. But his four adult children struggled to find jobs that paid a living wage. In 1998, Procopio's two oldest children headed north, willing to take their chances as undocumented immigrants in hope of a better life in the United States. However, the family hated being apart.

Two years later, Procopio's wife and their two younger children emigrated, too. Procopio remained in Mexico until he retired. Then, he got a 10-year tourist visa and joined his family.

Eventually, one of Procopio's sons married an American woman and became a U.S. citizen. Because Procopio had previously been inspected and granted entry to the country on a legal visa, he was able to adjust his immigration status from that of a tourist to a lawful permanent resident. Procopio's son, as a new American citizen, sponsored him. This was not the case for Procopio's wife, Cristina, who did not enter the United States on a legal visa. Her story is more tragic, as you will learn in a later chapter.

All immigrants must be sponsored by a United States citizen or lawful permanent resident. Sponsors must prove they have a genuine relationship with the immigrant, must make a certain level of income, and must promise to financially support the immigrant. Procopio became the pastor of a Hispanic congregation in the Midwest and lives near his children and 15 grandchildren.

IDENTITY NEWS

Procopio's immigration story is common. Most of the 1 million green cards distributed each year go to immediate relatives of U.S. citizens. The government does not limit how many immediate relatives a citizen can sponsor. Immediate relatives are not counted in the nation's annual worldwide immigration cap of 675,000 people.

A naturalization ceremony at the Grand Canyon

credit: National Park Service photo by Michael Quinn

Extended relatives of citizens or lawful permanent residents fall into a separate "family preference" category and are treated differently. Relatives such as adult siblings and unmarried adult children of citizens and lawful permanent residents are counted against the annual immigration cap.

Also, no single country can send more than 7 percent of the total number of immigrants the United States will accept each year. So, people from a country with lots of people waiting for family preference visas might wait years for their turn to emigrate. For people unwilling to wait that long, having a work skill offers another way to enter the United States.

SKILLED WORKERS

B.P. was born on St. Lucia, an emerald island in the Caribbean. In 2000, he rode on the winds of a hurricane to the United States. Well, sort of.

When a powerful storm devastated St. Lucia, a nonprofit organization run by the Catholic Church in Philadelphia went to the island to help rebuild, and B.P. volunteered with the group. When the priest in charge witnessed the young man's talent and energy, he asked B.P. to come to Philadelphia to work with the homeless. B.P. was only 18 and had never considered emigrating. But, eager for a challenge, he accepted the church's sponsorship and was granted a work visa.

The labor of immigrants has propelled the United States into the economic powerhouse it is today. After family reunification, the next priority of immigration law is to coax skilled immigrants to America's shores. Up to 140,000 immigrants can move to the United States each year for permanent jobs if they fit certain criteria.

Because the U.S. economy needs far more than 140,000 immigrants to keep it running smoothly, many thousands of foreign workers are admitted each year on temporary nonimmigrant employment visas. Technology giants such as Amazon and Microsoft sponsor high-tech experts. Hotels, construction companies, and commercial farms depend on seasonal workers when they cannot hire enough Americans.

Temporary employment visas require immigrants to return home when their visas expire. However, plans can change. More than half of the green cards the USCIS grants each year go to people already in the United States on temporary visas who apply for a status adjustment. Such was the case for B.P.

After working with Philadelphia's homeless for three years, B.P. was granted a student visa so he could remain in the United States to attend college. While in school, he fell in love and married an American woman. Although St. Lucia was still home in many ways, B.P. was now also tied to the United States. With his wife as his sponsor, B.P. became a lawful permanent resident.

The United States invited B.P. through the Golden Door because of his skills. Procopio was allowed in due to family ties.

Immigrant agricultural workers dig up sweet potatoes in a field in Virginia.

credit: USDA photo by Lance Cheung

REFUGEE AND ASYLUM

Some immigrants arrive at America's doorstep because their home countries are too dangerous. However, immigration law permits only a few to enter.

Watch "Still the Most Shocking Second a Day," a short video about one day in the life of a child refugee. How did this child's refugee experience change her?

still most shocking second

On March 25, 2018, a caravan of 1,000 migrants in southern Mexico began to walk north. Most of these men, women, and children were Honduran. Desperate to escape Honduras's violent streets, they marched 1,400 miles to the U.S. border, hoping to be granted asylum.

These Central American migrants are not unique. In 2017, the United Nations (UN) reported that 65.6 million people around the world had been forced to flee their homes because of persecution, conflict, or violence. This is a record high. About 22.5 million of these displaced people are refugees and another 2.3 million are asylum seekers.

The legal meaning of these words is the difference between life and death.

The Refugee Convention of 1951 is a United Nations treaty that spells out what it means to be legally regarded as a refugee. According to this multinational agreement, refugees are people who have fled their country. The UN or the government of a country must grant people refugee status for them to be protected under international law. Once that protection is granted, governments are forbidden from returning refugees to their home countries, and the UN places the refugees in temporary camps or resettles them in another country.

Asylum seekers are people who have fled their country for the same reasons as refugees, but their claim for protection has not yet been legally recognized by the UN or a national government. That claim might never be recognized. Although every refugee begins as an asylum seeker, not every asylum seeker is given the protected status of a refugee.

Of all the ways to legally enter the United States, coming in with refugee status is the hardest. After people flee their homeland, they can register with the UN or apply for asylum at a U.S. border checkpoint. Applicants must describe the harm they face at home and provide letters, medical reports, or photographs to prove their claim. Few asylum seekers have these documents. They have usually fled dangerous situations in a panic with few belongings.

> Gabriela Hernandez, one of the immigrants in the caravan from Honduras, proves this point.

The 27-year-old pregnant mother of two young sons divorced her abusive husband when she was still living in Honduras. Gang members tracked her down, demanding to know where her ex-husband was. Gabriela did not know. The gang told her she had 12 hours to discover his location or they would return and kill her six-year-old son. That night, Gabriela fled Honduras with her children. All they took were the clothes on their backs.[2]

Asylum seekers who arrive at the border are housed in detention centers while they await a decision on their request for refugee status. If approved, these immigrants are allowed to remain in the country and can apply for a green card in one year. If their claim is denied, they are deported.

Immigrants who live on other continents apply directly to the UN for asylum. The UN does background checks on all applicants, checking biometrics and fingerprint databases to ensure no criminals or terrorists are hiding among the desperate migrants.

GLOBAL SNAPSHOT: REFUGEE CRISIS

One-third of the world's 22.5 million refugees are Syrians forced out of their country by a brutal civil war. Ethnic violence in East Africa and conflict between terrorists and the government in Afghanistan are two other main causes of the global migration crisis. Most refugees are not resettled in wealthy countries such as the United States. When people flee danger at home, they usually stop in the closest neighboring country that is stable. Often, poor and middle-income nations bear the greatest burden of caring for displaced people. Turkey is hosting 2.5 million Syrian refugees, whereas, as of January 2018, the United States had accepted only 33,000.[3]

The Za'atri camp in Jordan for Syrian refugees in 2013

credit: U.S. Department of State

Refugees slated for resettlement do not get to choose what country they go to. The UN considers the refugee's culture, the location of any relatives, and the number of refugees each host country will take. When the UN wants to resettle refugees in the United States, the State Department vets these people again, a process that takes 18 to 24 months.

Presidents, with congressional approval, have the power to set the annual refugee limit. In 1990, the United States admitted 120,000 refugees. In 2016, President Obama (1961–) set the ceiling at 85,000. When President Trump (1946–) took office in 2017, he capped the number at 50,000 and in 2018, he lowered it further to 45,000.[4] Given the current state of immigration, how few refugees the United States accepts each year, and how long it takes to vet refugees, one might question whether the United States is violating the Refugee Convention, an international law the country signed onto back in 1951.

Gabriela Hernandez and the caravan of asylum seekers reached Tijuana, Mexico, on April 25, 2018. Hernandez could see the United States across the border fence. Although the woman understood that she and her children could be held in a detention facility for months, she planned to turn herself over to immigration officials and ask for asylum. If the United States refused to grant it, "I don't know what I'm going to do," Gabriela said. "I cannot go back to my country."

CITIZENSHIP

Those immigrants fortunate enough to get lawful permanent residency status can apply for citizenship once they have lived in the United States for a certain number of years. But before citizenship is granted, immigrants must pass a naturalization test. Procopio applied for citizenship as soon as he was eligible and began to study.

The day of his naturalization test, Procopio drove to the nearest USCIS office. When an immigration agent called Procopio's name, he followed the agent to an interview room. First, the agent questioned Procopio in English about his background. This was not random conversation.

> The agent was assessing Procopio's ability to understand and speak English.

Then, Procopio took a U.S. civics and history test. Applicants are given a 100-question practice test ahead of time. On the day of the test, the immigration officials ask only 10 questions picked at random. "I like history," Procopio said, "so I learned the answers to all 100 questions, first in Spanish and then in English."

Take the civics practice test to see if you would qualify to become a U.S. citizen.

🔍 USCIS
practice test

The last hurdle Procopio had to overcome was to read aloud one sentence in English and write one sentence in English. Procopio's preparation paid off. He aced the test.

Procopio's journey to citizenship ended at a public ceremony at the Milwaukee, Wisconsin, courthouse, where a federal judge administered the citizenship oath. Along with a group of other immigrants, Procopio vowed to give up loyalty to other countries and to uphold and defend the United States.

With this promise, Procopio was no longer an immigrant. He assumed the mantle of a U.S. citizen with all its rights and responsibilities.

WALL, DRONES, AND GUARDS

Immigration law can secure the Golden Door only if it is enforced. Keeping undocumented immigrants out of the country is the job of ICE and CBP. These federal agencies are part of the U.S. Department of Homeland Security, the unit of the federal government that secures the nation's borders and enforces immigration law in the country's interior.

The border between the United States and Mexico stretches from the Pacific Ocean to the Gulf of Mexico. Rivers, canyons, and desert form a natural barrier that the U.S. government is reinforcing with walls and fences.

In the 1990s, the federal government erected a 66-mile wall between Tijuana and San Diego. The Secure Fence Act of 2006 added another 450 miles of barrier. In 2016, Donald Trump campaigned for president and vowed to "build a great, great wall on our southern border and . . . have Mexico pay for that wall."[5]

BORDER ZONE/ DANGER ZONE

Customs and Border Patrol agents have broad powers in the "no-man's land" that circles the United States and extends 100 air miles into the nation's interior, including parts of New York City, Philadelphia, Chicago, and all of Michigan and Florida. In this zone, agents can enter private land without a search warrant, set up checkpoints, inspect vehicles, and question anyone they suspect of being an undocumented immigrant.

Mexico will not foot the bill for Trump's border wall and Congress is also reluctant to pay for it. As of 2018, plans for the border wall include 700 miles of fencing. Estimates to build a barrier along the entire border run as high as $67 billion. In March 2018, Congress budgeted $1.6 billion for increased border security, but this money was earmarked for fencing, planning, and technology upgrades.[6] Trump's wall might never be built.

There is, however, a "human" border wall. In 2006, CBP had 11,032 agents along the southern border. This increased by 54 percent in 2016. And, in 2017, President Trump authorized the hiring of another 5,000 people, according to the Brookings Institute.

IDENTITY NEWS

In the last 15 years, fewer undocumented immigrants have been arrested trying to enter the United States on the southern border. In 2000, 1.6 million people were arrested. By 2017, arrests had declined by 82 percent.[7]

The fence between the United States and Mexico along the Pacific Ocean just south of San Diego

credit: Tony Webster (CC BY 2.0)

Technology forms a less-visible, but effective, border wall. Immigration agents sit in portable sheds in border towns, their computers linked to surveillance equipment aimed at the Mexican side of the Rio Grande River. These agents relay information to men in the field positioned to catch migrants when they step on U.S. soil. Towers topped with radar scan the horizon. Drones, blimps, and helicopters hover overhead, and more than 10,000 sensors trigger alerts from underground.

FIRE AND ICE

At 9 a.m. on April 5, 2018, shouts rang throughout a meatpacking plant in Morristown, Tennessee. "Inmigración! Inmigración!" The 100 workers, most Latino immigrants, panicked.

People bolted for the exits only to find them blocked by ICE agents. Some workers wedged themselves between hanging cow carcasses, and one man hid inside a walk-in freezer.

ICE agents quickly rounded up and handcuffed all the Latino workers. Some immigrants with young children or medical conditions were given orders to appear before a judge at a later date. The rest were sent to detention facilities to await deportation proceedings.

Workplace raids are an old strategy in the immigration enforcement playbook. During George W. Bush's presidency, ICE conducted large-scale raids that resulted in the deportation of thousands of workers. Initially, these raids continued under President Obama, but then his administration switched to less-visible enforcement. Under Obama, ICE conducted "silent raids" by auditing employers' records and fining them if they hired undocumented workers.

SOCIAL SECURITY

Citizens and lawful permanent residents pay taxes into the Social Security fund. When they retire, they get this money back as a monthly support check. Undocumented immigrant workers using false documents also pay taxes, including $13 billion annually to Social Security. However, they will never collect a penny of this when they retire. Does this seem fair to you? Do you think undocumented immigrants have a right to the same support systems, or do they waive that right when they illegally cross the border?

When President Trump took office in 2017, he vowed to vigorously enforce all immigration laws. Between October 2017 and May 2018, ICE conducted 3,410 workplace raids, double the number from the previous year.[8] The administration was determined to prosecute undocumented immigrants for "identity theft" and "document forging." Workers must provide a Social Security number when first hired, but immigrants in the country illegally are not allowed to apply for one. Instead, they forge a Social Security card or use someone else's.

THE DEPORTATION MACHINE

One October night in 2017, doctors at the medical center in Laredo, Texas, transferred 10-year-old Rosamaria Hernandez to a hospital in Corpus Christi for emergency gall bladder surgery. Rosamaria has cerebral palsy. The girl's undocumented parents dared not accompany her because the route to the hospital passed an immigration checkpoint.

Border Patrol agents stopped the ambulance on its way to the hospital, demanding to see Rosamaria's papers. When they discovered she was undocumented, agents followed the ambulance to the hospital and sat outside Rosamaria's room.

> When doctors released her, immigration agents immediately took Rosamaria to a detention facility 100 miles from her home.

Rosamaria was apprehended in a border town, but the 11.1 million undocumented immigrants in the United States can be arrested anywhere. In 2016, the number of deportation arrests jumped by 42 percent.[9]

"Drawings by Themselves: Portraits of America" is a multimedia project by which detained immigrants share their experiences through art. Listen to the story of a 16-year-old Honduran girl. What does her art reveal about the challenges she faced in coming to the United States?

🔍 endisolation portraits video

In 1996, an average of 8,500 people were in immigration detention on any given day. At the end of 2016, the average had reached 40,000 people a day, a record high.[11]

KEY QUESTIONS

- Is a physical wall an effective way of keeping undocumented immigrants out of the United States? Why might technology work better?

- What rights do you think an undocumented immigrant should be granted when in the United States?

- What, if anything, should the U.S. government do to help refugees and asylum seekers? Why?

When ICE arrests an undocumented immigrant, the agency has several options. Officials might allow the person to "voluntarily deport." This means immigrants who agree are given a few weeks to get their affairs in order and then must leave the country. ICE can also choose to release immigrants from detention on bail until their court dates. If the immigrants cannot afford the bail bond, they stay locked up. In 2018, the U.S. Supreme Court ruled that, under current law, immigrants do not have the right to a hearing to determine if they are eligible to be released on bond. ICE can authorize it or not.

Many immigrants remain in detention an average of two years until their deportation hearing.

When immigrants get their day in court, a federal immigration judge hears evidence on the case. Immigrants do not have the right to a court-appointed attorney. If the judge rules against an immigrant, the immigrant can appeal, but must remain in detention until the case is resolved. If the appeal is lost, the immigrant is deported to their country of origin.

For some people, that means an airplane flight—for others, a bus ride. In 2016, each deportation cost ICE $10,854. That year the agency deported 240,000 people.[12]

Given the challenges of immigrating legally and the risks of undocumented immigration, why don't people just stay in the countries where they were born? In the next chapter, we'll look at why immigrants leave their homelands and what they are willing to endure to reach America.

GRAFFITI AS PROTEST

Throughout history, politicians have constructed walls to protect or divide, and people have created art on those walls to rebel and resist. In this activity, you will design art for a segment of the U.S.-Mexican border wall that reflects your opinion of the state of immigration in the twenty-first century.

- **Research different views of President Trump's proposed border wall.** Read the opinions of both Republican and Democratic lawmakers, economic analysts, environmental experts, immigration officials, and immigrant advocates.

- **Decide what you think about the border wall.** Is it needed? How much will it cost? How effective will it be? What does an extended border wall say about the United States? What are the psychological impacts of living behind a wall?

- **Write a thesis statement to communicate your main opinion of the border wall.** A thesis statement is usually a single sentence that summarizes your specific position on a subject.

- **Brainstorm different ways you can artistically represent your thesis.** How will you execute your ideas?

- **Draw, paint, or sketch your ideas on a large piece of butcher paper.** Display on a fence or wall so people can view your artistic expression.

> **To investigate more,** research examples of border wall graffiti on walls around the world. What common themes or images are reflected by artists in different countries?

VOCAB LAB

Write down what you think each word means. What root words can you find to help you? What does the context of the word tell you?

asylum, **audit**, **background check**, **bail**, **biometrics**, **displaced**, **psychological**, and **United Nations**.

Compare your definitions with those of your friends or classmates. Did you all come up with the same meanings? Turn to the text and glossary if you need help.

BORDER POETRY

Albert Rios (1952–), Arizona's poet laureate from 2013 to 2015, is the author of a double sonnet poem titled "The Border." This is the beginning of the poem.

The border is a line that birds cannot see

The border is a beautiful piece of paper folded carelessly in half

The border is where flint first met steel, starting a century of fires

The border is a belt that is too tight, holding things up but making it hard to breathe.

- **Find Albert's poem in a book or online and read the whole thing.** What does Rios compare the U.S.-Mexico border to?

- **Draw or photocopy a map of your school.** What kinds of borders, visible or invisible, exist in your school? Do cliques sit at certain tables in the cafeteria? Are some places the unspoken territory of a particular group of students?

- **Reflect on these borders.** How do new students learn about their existence? What happens when a student tries to cross a border? What forces hold these borders up or break them down? Do these borders help you or hurt you?

- **Using "The Border" as a model, write a poem about your school.** Share your poem with friends, classmates, or teachers. Do they recognize the same borders as you?

To investigate more, locate poems by other authors that describe borders, un-crossable lines, or walls. Rewrite your poem in the style of another poet. How does the meaning or mood change?

Chapter 3
The Push and the Pull

YOU KNOW, THERE REALLY ARE A LOT OF MISCONCEPTIONS ABOUT IMMIGRATION.

What drives migrants to leave their homelands?

Some immigrants are desperate for safety and security, some are seeking economic opportunity, and still others want to be with their families. Immigrants leave their homes for many different reasons.

A stream ran in front of the house where José Luis Zelaya grew up in a barrio of San Pedro Sula, Honduras. Women washed clothes in the creek and children fished in it, but the water also washed up the dead—both animal and human. Violence was as common as the chickens that ran through the streets, and José was used to the echo of gunfire.

An abusive father brought the violence of the streets into José's home and poverty made escape difficult. When José's mother tried to flee with him and his little sister, her husband stopped her, usually with his fists. Finally, when José was 11 years old, an uncle helped his mother get away, but she could take only one of her children. Because José was older, he stayed behind. His mother planned to find a job in the United States and save every penny so she could send for José as soon as possible.

José endured his father's abuse and the violence of his neighborhood. One day, while playing soccer, José was shot in the arm during a gang drive-by.

> With no money to pay a doctor,
> he tended the wounds himself.

Migrants are both pushed out of their homes and pulled toward a specific place. For José, poverty and violence made life unendurable in Honduras. His mother and sister were what drew him toward the United States. When telling his story to a reporter many years later, José said, "I wanted to come to the U.S. because my mother was here. I honestly was not coming here for any other reason but to reunify with my mother and my sister."[1]

During the last 70 years, the countries from which immigrants come to the United States have changed dramatically. However, the core reasons people leave their homelands is the same. Immigrants seek economic opportunity and security.

Let's look at the emigration stories of people from different regions of the world.

IDENTITY NEWS

In 1960, 84 percent of immigrants came from Canada and Europe. Then, in 1965, the Immigration and Nationality Act opened the door to non-European immigration. By 2015, most newly arrived immigrants were from Asia. And more immigrants arrived from sub-Saharan Africa, the Caribbean, South and Central America, and the Middle East than earlier in U.S. history.

Street graffiti in a Honduran city

ASIA

Asians represent the fastest-growing ethnic group in the United States, and most of this growth is due to immigration. In 1960, only 491,000 Asian immigrants were in the country. By 2014, there were 12.8 million, an increase of 2,597 percent! Most Asian immigrants come from six countries—China, the Philippines, India, Vietnam, Korea, and Japan.

Many Asians come to the United States on employment visas.

A 10-year United States B visa issued to a Chinese citizen

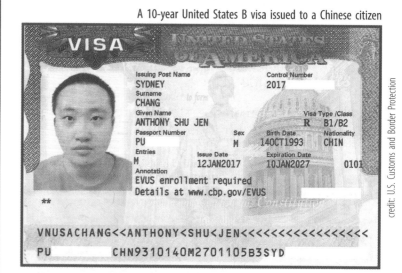

credit: U.S. Customs and Border Protection

Tulip Nandu was one such immigrant. In 2010, when he was 24 years old, Tulip came to the United States from India to get his second master's degree. He had relatives who had studied in America, and he knew the country offered some of the best programs in his field of bioinformatics. Although he had never visited the United States before, Tulip said, "It was an easy choice." He lived a pampered life in India and wanted to see what he could do on his own.

View a video about four Filipino women planning to emigrate to the United States. What factors are pushing them from their homeland? What factors are pulling them toward the United States?

PBS worth it

Money and an education in a valued field were the tickets Tulip needed to enter the United States legally. He traveled in comfort on a plane, earned his degree, and was hired by a medical center in Texas, where he is working on yet another advanced degree. Tulip described the United States as "a country of opportunities" where an immigrant willing to work hard would "reap the benefits."[2]

Many Asian immigrants have stories similar to Tulip's. A 2012 survey of Asians living in the United States found that 73 percent of them believed the United States gave them a better chance to "get ahead" than their home countries did.

Not all Asians come through legal channels as Tulip did, however. Although the stereotype of an undocumented immigrant is a Mexican crossing the southern border, Asians are the fastest-growing group of undocumented immigrants. Most arrive in the United States legally on tourist or student visas and do not go home when their visas expire.

LATIN AMERICA

Since 2009, more Mexicans have been leaving the United States than entering, and South America does not send many immigrants to the United States.[3] The upsurge of Latin American immigrants in recent years is due to events in Central America.

The Northern Triangle of Central America is a dangerous and economically poor place to live. According to researchers, immigration from El Salvador, Honduras, and Guatemala, the three countries that make up the triangle, increased 25 percent between 2007 and 2015.

IDENTITY NEWS

Between 2009 and 2014, 1 million Mexican immigrants living in the United States returned home, a net loss of 140,000.[4]

POVERTY

Poverty pushes Guatemalans to migrate. Sixty percent of the population lives on less than $1.90 per day. Half of the population is under age 19. Of the 140,000 youth that enter the labor market each year, only two out of 10 will find work. Left with few options, Guatemalans head north in search of a better life.[5]

José Zelaya's experience in Honduras illustrates the challenges of living in a country plagued by violence. Neighboring El Salvador is no better. In this country of 6.5 million people, half a million are involved with gangs.

According to *The Wall Street Journal*, in 2018, El Salvador has the highest murder rate in the world.

Most of the victims in El Salvador are young men from poor urban neighborhoods, but the gangs are increasingly targeting girls for sexual violence. Gang members strike at rivals by raping or killing their sisters.

As a result, the young in El Salvador have a terrible choice. They can remain in their homeland and face violence and death every day. Or they can embark on the risky journey north in the hopes that the United States will grant them asylum.

MIDDLE EAST AND AFRICA

Armed conflict erupted in the Middle East in 2011, causing millions of people to flee their homes. Most sought shelter in neighboring countries, but by 2016, some 810,000 immigrants had arrived in the United States. Half came through family sponsorships and another 30 percent as refugees.[6]

Immigration from Africa is also on the rise as conflict pushes people to seek safety. In 2000, only 881,000 African immigrants lived in the United States. By 2015, that number had climbed to 2.1 million. In 2015, the U.S. State Department reported that of the top 10 countries sending refugees, four were in Africa.

Somalia is one of these African nations, a country that experts label a "fragile state." Between 1990 and 2015, the number of Somalian migrants increased by 136 percent. Many made the dangerous journey over land and sea to Europe, while others remained in refugee camps in neighboring Kenya or Ethiopia.

Abdi Nor wanted desperately to immigrate to the United States. Since childhood, he had been obsessed with the United States, mastering English without an accent by watching American movies. His friends even nicknamed him "Abdi the American."

Abdi was only six years old when civil war erupted in Somalia. For years, Somalia had no functioning government as rival warlords and armed militia battled for control of territory. The terrorist group al-Shabaab attacked people and bombed buildings, and members pressured young men like Abdi either to join their ranks or be killed.

> Abdi fled to neighboring Kenya, where he lived without legal authorization in a neighborhood of other Somali refugees.

Life in this slum, where food was scarce and jobs nonexistent, might have been Abdi's future, but he got lucky. Every fall, in countries around the world, signs go up advertising the U.S. Diversity Visa Program. This lottery program distributes 55,000 green cards to people from countries with historically low migration to the United States. Between 8 and 15 million people apply each year, and in 2014, Abdi entered and won. He was eligible to apply for a permanent resident visa to America, the land of his dreams.

In 2014, more than 68,000 unaccompanied minors were apprehended crossing the U.S.-Mexican border. Most were from Central America. View the maps of where they came from and where some have been settled.

NYT questions border kids

A rusting tank in the Somalian desert

credit: Carl Montgomery (CC BY 2.0)

DANGEROUS JOURNEYS

Each person's immigration journey is unique. When Abdi Nor's name was drawn in the diversity lottery, the American dream was within his reach. But because Somalia was in such chaos, Abdi's emigration was a nightmare.

Challenging hurdles blocked Abdi's way out of Somalia. He had to gather documents such as medical records and school transcripts, pass a criminal background check, and be interviewed by an official at the American embassy.

> "What kept us going was America," Abdi said. "America was the place I dreamed about—quite literally, every night."[8]

Locating the documents was difficult because Abdi was living illegally and under the government's radar in Kenya. He and his brother shared a one-room apartment and sold socks on the street to raise money for food while they attended college classes.

Only weeks before his scheduled interview at the embassy, al-Shabaab terrorists held hundreds of hostages in a Kenyan mall for days, eventually killing 67 people. Because al-Shabaab is a terrorist group from Somalia, Kenyan police began to round up Somali refugees and hold them in detention.

On April 17, 2004, the police came to the apartment where Abdi was living. One officer grabbed Abdi by the shirt. "Come with me," he ordered.

Abdi knew if he wound up in detention, he would not be released in time for his interview at the U.S. embassy, scheduled for July 22. If he missed the interview, he would lose his chance to pass through America's Golden Door.

Abdi showed the officer his UN refugee ID tag, but the man ignored it. So, Abdi and his friends pooled their money together and came up with $80.

Watch a short video of Honduran youth explaining why they chose to emigrate. With young people facing the kind of struggles described in this video, should the United States grant them asylum when they arrive at the border?

WOLA children under threat

"Please," Abdi begged the officer, "That's all I have in life . . . . Please, you have to take it."

The cop took the bribe, but this was no guarantee that another police officer would not return the next day and demand more money. So, Abdi went into hiding. He and his brother shared their food with another Somali family in their apartment building. Soon, they were eating just a little bit of bread, tea, and sugar each day.

For his interview, Abdi needed to get a certificate of good conduct from the Kenyan police stating that he was not a criminal. But he was too terrified to walk into what he saw as the lion's den.

Finally, as the date of the interview loomed ever closer, Abdi screwed up his courage and went to the police headquarters. To his surprise, he ran into bureaucracy, not brutality. The officer told Abdi the certificate he needed had to be processed through the UN and could take up to five months. That would be too late to do him any good.

Abdi did not give up. Every week, he returned to police headquarters and asked for the certificate, hoping to get a different answer. Days passed in boredom and nights in terror. Kenyan police kept banging on doors in Abdi's neighborhood looking for Somalians. Abdi blackened his windows and remained silent until the pounding ceased. "You know, they are killing us. They are killing us with fear," Abdi told an American journalist who was following his case.

Finally, on May 29, the Kenyan police gave Abdi the clearance document he needed. "I smell the U.S. visa," Abdi told the reporter. "I smell it. I smell it." His mood changed from despair to being "in love with everything."

GLOBAL SNAPSHOT: DEATH AT SEA

The number of African and Asian migrants attempting to cross the Mediterranean Sea to reach Europe has dropped by 94 percent from its peak in 2015. But the proportion of migrants dying in their effort to emigrate is rising. In the first six months of 2018, 28 out of every 1,000 migrants died. Because surrounding countries have cooperated to close off various paths to Europe, migrants are left with the most dangerous route—across the central Mediterranean from Libya to Italy. Sometimes, migrants can be stranded at sea for weeks.[9]

Abdi's journey was not yet over. He went to the embassy on the appointed day. Legs shaking and heart pounding, he handed all his documents to the American official. She scanned them and then looked up at Abdi.

"The transcript that you have here does not have a signature," she said. "Sorry, I can't give you the visa." Then, she stood to bring in the next applicant.

Abdi was stunned. He went outside and sat under a tree in the embassy yard, holding his head in his hands. "I was looking at this whole world as the worst place to live," he said.

The official had told Abdi he could send in a signed transcript, and maybe, just maybe, the Americans would get in touch with him. So, Abdi got the transcript signed and mailed it in. But he was convinced he had missed his chance.

Two days passed, and Abdi heard no news. Then four days, seven days, nine days. Still silence.

Kenya is suffering from a refugee crisis. In this photo, workers from the UN gather bundles of shelters and mosquito nets that have been dropped from a cargo plane.

credit: Robert Palomares, U.S. Navy

Finally, on the 10th day, Abdi got an email from the embassy—his visa was in the mail. He leaped onto his bed and jumped for joy.

On August 11, 2014, Abdi flew from Nairobi, Kenya, to begin his new life in America. He settled in Maine. As of June 2018, Abdi was working as a Somali interpreter with plans to attend college and study political science. He wrote a memoir about his experiences called *Call Me American*.

THE TRAIL OF AN UNDOCUMENTED IMMIGRANT

Millions of people immigrate to the United States without a visa. The dangerous journeys they are willing to undertake are evidence of how desperate they are to escape their homelands.

During the two years that José Luis Zelaya had been dodging his father's fists and gang gunfire in Honduras, his mother had been in the United States selling tamales, cleaning houses, and babysitting. She saved every cent until she earned the $7,600 needed to pay smugglers to bring her son north.

José's grandmother helped him escape his father's house and took him to Guatemala. José said goodbye to his grandmother, uncertain if they would ever see each other again.

The smugglers, called coyotes, first took José and the other migrants to a brothel that stank of urine and feces. The smugglers taught the migrants, many of them children, to communicate by whistling. Once they crossed the border into Mexico, the coyotes did not want the children's accents to give away their nationalities. Mexican gangs prey on migrants from Central America.

Go to the Arizona OpenGIS Initiative for Deceased Migrants website to investigate the deaths of migrants who crossed the border between Arizona and Mexico. What can you conclude about whether border crossing has become safer or more dangerous between 2000 and 2018? What might explain the low number of female migrants dying compared to males? What seems to be the main cause of death of these immigrants?

Arizona deceased migrants

Buses took the migrants only so far and then they had to walk. They slept by day and walked by night so Mexican immigration authorities would not catch them. Snakes and scorpions lurked in their path. One by one, José's toenails fell off. Despite the constant hunger, the thought of seeing his sister and mother again kept José going.

When they finally reached the border, the coyotes organized the travelers into small groups, partnering José up with a girl who was supposed to pretend to be his sister. José was unaware he would be breaking U.S. law when he crossed the border. "We're just children . . . trying to find our parents."

The coyotes dropped the migrants off at a narrow stretch of the Rio Grande River, and a smuggler accompanied the children as they swam to Texas. When they climbed up on the riverbank, the coyote told everyone to scram. Soon, José was alone.

Exhausted, he lay down and slept. When he awoke the next day, José walked until he ran into a Border Patrol agent. The agent took José to a nearby detention center. Eventually, he was reunited with his mother and sister in Texas and was allowed to remain in the United States under the Deferred Action for Childhood Arrivals Act. As of late 2018, José was working as a motivational speaker while pursuing his doctorate in urban education at Texas A&M University. José hopes to return to Honduras in the future. His goal is to become the secretary of education and help reform the country's education system.

Some immigrants find the United States a friendly and welcoming country. Others encounter hostility and racism. The next chapter will explore the experience of immigrants after they pass through the Golden Door.

KEY QUESTIONS

- How are immigrant experiences different depending on where they originate from and why they leave their countries? How are immigrant experiences similar?

- Should the U.S. government create different immigration laws for people coming from different countries, or should all immigration laws address all immigrants, no matter their countries of origin?

HUMAN RIGHTS DENIED

What are human rights? What is the relationship between human rights and immigration policies in the United States?

- **Make a list of the rights you believe all human beings should have.** These are rights that race, ethnicity, sex, or any status should not affect.

- **In 1948, the UN adopted the Universal Declaration of Human Rights.** Read the plain language version of this declaration and compare it to your list. UN human rights

- **Choose the human right you believe most people are seeking when they decide to emigrate.** Use the internet, a newspaper, or magazine to locate the story of a person who emigrated for reasons related to the human right you chose.

- **Create a visual representation of how this human right was restricted or denied to this immigrant in his or her homeland.** Post the visual for others to see and ask them how relevant this human right is in their daily lives.

> **To investigate more,** compare the rights listed in the UN Universal Declaration of Human Rights with the rights guaranteed in the U.S. Constitution. How are they similar? How do they differ? Are any important rights not included in either document? Should immigration be considered a fundamental human right?

VOCAB LAB

Write down what you think each word means. What root words can you find to help you? What does the context of the word tell you?

barrio, brothel, bureaucracy, coyote, migrant, militia, and **stereotype**.

Compare your definitions with those of your friends or classmates. Did you all come up with the same meanings? Turn to the text and glossary if you need help.

A BALSERO BOAT

More than 1 million Cubans have immigrated to the United States since Cuba's communist revolution in 1959. Although the Cuban government usually prohibits its citizens from emigrating, many people escape the island on homemade vessels fashioned from inner tubes, wood, ropes, and old car parts. These balseros, or rafters, brave the 90-mile sea voyage to Florida.

- **Design a boat that can paddle itself across a container of water using a rubber band as a power source.** Brainstorm and design your boat.

  - How will you construct your boat so it does not sink, leak, or roll over? What kind of materials can you use?

  - What materials make the best paddles, and what shape and size should they be?

  - How will you attach the paddles to the boat so they are free to turn without falling off?

  - How will you fashion a frame to hold your paddles and rubber band engine?

- **Perform a test run and modify your boat.**

  - After building your boat, test it in a kiddie pool or bathtub.

  - Can you modify your design to make your boat faster or more stable? What happens if you design the boat so the paddles turn partly in the air and partly in water? If they are fully immersed in water? If they turn above the water's surface? What happens if you use more than one rubber band or twist the rubber band?

> **To investigate more,** research the migration of people across the Mediterranean Sea to Europe. Why is this crossing so deadly? What kind of boats do migrants travel on? How heavily loaded are they? How do weather conditions in the Mediterranean Sea compare with those of the Florida Strait the Cuban migrants travel to get to the United States?

Chapter 4

The Welcome Mat

YOU KNOW, JUST WALKING AROUND TOWN...

How do native-born Americans view immigrants?

Different people have different views on immigrants and immigration policy. As the U.S. government struggles to initiate policies and plans that benefit everyone, people express their views through different channels.

Shortly after immigrating to the United States, Pastor Procopio, the immigrant from Mexico we learned about in Chapter 2, was out shopping when the sky opened up and rain poured down. Procopio hunched up his shoulders, preparing to get soaked, when suddenly a stranger appeared at his side, an umbrella in the man's outstretched hand. This kindness affirmed Procopio's feeling that immigration had been the right decision.

However, Procopio's wife, Cristina, has not always felt welcomed. She has been ignored by clerks and heard racist comments muttered by waiters. When asked to explain their different perceptions of how immigrants are received in America, Procopio can only shrug. "Not all people are good and not all people are bad," he said.

Good and bad—that sums up the reception immigrants receive in the United States.

PUBLIC PERCEPTION

A 2015 survey found that three-quarters of adults in the United States have immigrants in their neighborhoods, and 24 percent have a friend or relative who is a recent immigrant. Despite this, many native-born Americans stereotype people not born in this country. When asked to describe immigrants in one word, the word chosen most was "illegal."[1]

Despite this inaccurate and negative label, public perception of immigrants has improved in the twenty-first century. In 1994, a Pew Research Center survey found that 63 percent of Americans believed immigrants burdened the nation. In 2017, a similar survey found only 27 percent of respondents labeled immigrants as a burden, and 63 percent said they strengthened the United States.

Support for immigrants can be found around the country, often declared on signs during marches to protest restrictive immigration laws and practices.

credit: Molly Adams (CC BY 2.0)

President Obama said his administration would target, "criminals, gang bangers, people who are hurting the community, not . . . students, not . . . folks who are here just because they're trying to figure out how to feed their families."

President Obama delivers a speech on immigration reform at a high school in Las Vegas, Nevada.

credit: Official White House Photo by Pete Souza

A more positive public attitude toward immigrants does not always equal a warmer welcome from government officials. As head of the executive branch, the president is the nation's top law enforcer. Because the government has limited resources and there are millions of immigrants, the president sets priorities to guide how agents should enforce immigration laws.

Therefore, the reception immigrants get when they enter the country can look and feel very different depending on who is president.

DEPORTER IN CHIEF

From 2009 to 2017, President Barack Obama set three priorities for immigration enforcement.

1) Deport immigrants, legal or undocumented, considered threats to national security or public safety.

2) Deport undocumented immigrants who had recently crossed the border or were repeat offenders.

3) Think twice before arresting undocumented immigrants who were very young, very old, veterans, seriously ill, victims of domestic abuse or human trafficking, and who had long-term ties to the United States.

However, plenty of undocumented immigrants convicted of minor offenses were caught up in the immigration enforcement net while Obama was president. Between 2008 and 2014, two-thirds of the immigrants removed from the United States had either committed minor offenses or had no criminal record at all.[2] As a result, critics labeled Obama "deporter in chief."

One method of deporting an immigrant is when a judge issues an "order of removal." This order bans the immigrant from applying to reenter the United States for a certain number of years—it also means the person has a formal charge on his or her record. The Obama administration used this method to remove 3 million undocumented immigrants from the United States, compared to only 2 million removed by the administration of his predecessor, President George W. Bush.

RHETORIC AND ROUNDUPS

When Donald Trump announced his candidacy for president on June 16, 2015, some of his first words targeted immigrants. "When Mexico sends its people, they're not sending their best," Trump railed. "They're sending people that have lots of problems . . . . They're bringing drugs. They're bringing crime."[3]

credit: Charlotte Cuthbertson/The Epoch Times (CC BY 2.0)

To stop these immigrants, Trump promised to build a border wall and create a "deportation force" to remove the estimated 11 million undocumented immigrants living in the United States. A few months later, after a terrorist attack in San Bernardino, California, left 14 people dead, President Trump called for "a total and complete shutdown of Muslims entering the United States . . . ."[4] The San Bernardino terrorists were Muslim immigrants, and Trump took this as proof that Muslims should be barred from coming to America.

On November 8, 2016, Donald Trump was elected president of the United States. He began to work to fulfill his promise to reform the immigration system.

Under President Trump, major changes in U.S. immigration policy and enforcement have affected many people, including a woman named Maribel Trujillo Diaz. She came to the United States without documentation in 2002, settled in Ohio, and had four children, supporting her family by working in a candy factory. In 2012, Maribel filed for asylum because the area where she had lived in Mexico was controlled by violent drug cartels.

Maribel's appeal was denied, but ICE did not deport her. Instead, the agency granted her a one-year work permit and ordered her to check in regularly. Maribel believed that as long as she did as ICE asked, she could remain in the United States with her children.

On April 5, 2017, Maribel reported to the ICE office in Fairfield, Ohio, for her scheduled check-in. Two days later, a truck full of ICE agents pulled up beside her when she was out for a walk and arrested her. Within two weeks, she was back in Mexico. Her four young children, all American citizens, remained in the States.[5]

When President Trump's travel ban went into effect on January 28, 2017, protests erupted at airports across the country. View the gallery of photographs at this website. What do the protestors' signs reveal about their attitudes about immigration?

Daily Telegraph protests immigration Trump pictures 2017

TRAVEL BAN

One week after he took office, President Trump signed an executive order that suspended immigration from seven countries where most of the population was Muslim. The administration said this was a matter of national security because these countries did not screen visa applicants well enough. In his view, terrorists could slip into the country through security gaps.

> Opponents immediately challenged the ban in court, insisting the ban was based on prejudice against Muslims, not national security.

Lower courts declared the travel ban unconstitutional, so the government revised its wording. On June 26, 2018, the U.S. Supreme Court upheld the final version of the ban. As of the summer of 2018, citizens of Chad, Iran, Libya, North Korea, Somalia, Syria, Venezuela, and Yemen are barred from immigrating permanently to the United States. Some citizens of those countries are prohibited from working, studying, and vacationing here, too.

During the past year, the visa application process has become more complicated. Rather than a phone interview, applicants must undergo an in-person interview at a U.S. embassy. Those seeking an employment visa must provide 15 years of travel and job histories and turn over passwords to all social media accounts they have used during the last five years.

ICE ARRESTS

ICE has been empowered to reach deep into the nation's interior and arrest anyone without documentation. According to the Migration Policy Institute, between January 2017 and September 2017, the agency arrested 42 percent more people than it did in 2016 and removed 37 percent more immigrants from the central regions of the country. Of the 110,568 people arrested in 2017, almost 32,000 had no criminal convictions.

FAMILY SEPARATION

On May 7, 2018, U.S. Attorney General Jeff Sessions launched the "zero-tolerance" policy. Sessions warned immigrants crossing the U.S.-Mexico border, "If you are smuggling a child, then we will prosecute you, and that child will be separated from you as required by law."[6] However, in the spring of 2018, immigrants at the southern border were mostly Central American families seeking asylum, not human traffickers.

Border Patrol agents arrested many parents who crossed the border. They sent parents to detention centers and children to the U.S. Department of Health and Human Services Office of Refugee Resettlement. These children were placed in foster homes or facilities just for kids.

The zero-tolerance policy was in effect for two months. More than 2,300 families were separated. When Senator Jeff Merkley (1956–) was finally allowed to tour a children's detention facility in McCallum, Texas, he was appalled by the stark conditions. There were "hundreds of children locked up in cages," he said in a video. "Cages made out of fencing and . . . wire and nets stretched across the top of them so people can't climb out." Children lay on mattresses on concrete floors.

Anyone under age 12, including infants and toddlers, was housed in what the administration called "tender age shelters." Elizabeth Frankel, associate director of the Young Center for Immigrant Children's Rights, told a reporter for *The New York Times* that the children were "in crisis. They're just crying uncontrollably. We've seen young kids having panic attacks, they can't sleep, they're wetting the bed . . . . They may have been verbal, but now they can no longer talk."

Haitian immigrants protest immigration policies in 2018

credit: Fibonacci Blue (CC BY 2.0)

The family separations sparked an international outcry. At first, the administration defended its zero-tolerance strategy. But under mounting pressure, President Trump reversed the decision and signed an executive order to keep immigrant families together in detention.

Workplace raids. Family separation. Travel bans.

Immigrants in the United States feel anxious. Afraid of drawing attention to themselves, undocumented immigrants are reporting crimes less often than in previous years. Some do not apply for public assistance such as health care and food stamps for their American-born children.

Seydi Sarr, a green card holder from Senegal, feels targeted because of her Muslim faith. She has to explain to her children that Muslims are not terrorists and Islam is not a bad faith, because her children hear politicians say otherwise on the news. However, Seydi has also met Americans who are "totally giving and totally loving."[8] This is the other face of the United States.

FAMILIES BELONG TOGETHER

The policy of separating migrant families seeking asylum at the border sparked the Families Belong Together movement, a grassroots coalition of human rights and immigrant support organizations. On June 30, 2018, hundreds of thousands of protestors held rallies in 700 locations across the country. Do you think this protest had an effect on members of the government?

ROLL OUT THE WELCOME MAT

Even as the federal government changes immigration policies and practices, many Americans want the promise of Lady Liberty to remain true.

Nashville, Tennessee, is an example of a city working to build relationships between native-born Americans and newcomers. Between 1990 and 2014, Tennessee had a 400-percent increase in its immigrant population. Residents saw their city change rapidly as Mexican, Kurdish, and Somali immigrants moved next door. When cultural change happens quickly, people sometimes become less generous—and less trustful. In Nashville, someone set fire to a local mosque and a councilman introduced an English-only law.

To counteract this xenophobia, David Lubell, the head of the Tennessee Immigrant and Refugee Rights Coalition, created Welcoming Tennessee. The group organized community dinners, church gatherings, and talks at local organizations. Members put up billboards with positive messages about immigrants and trained volunteer ambassadors to bring people together from different ethnic and racial backgrounds. Regular meetings led to constructive conversations.

Welcoming Tennessee made a difference. Between 2006 and 2008, attitudes toward immigrants improved. The English-only measure was defeated by a wide margin, and a 2013 poll showed that three-quarters of people in Tennessee supported a path to citizenship for undocumented immigrants.[9] David decided to expand this successful program, and in 2009, he founded Welcoming America, a nationwide version of the Tennessee model.

TOP 10

In 2017, *US News & World Report* surveyed 21,000 people around the world about the economic stability, job prospects, income equality, and living conditions of 80 countries. Then editors ranked the top 10 countries that are the best places for immigrants. The results?

#10 Denmark
#9 Finland
#8 Netherlands
#7 United States
#6 Norway
#5 Germany
#4 Australia
#3 Switzerland
#2 Canada

And the winner is . . .
#1 Sweden

Organizations similar to this are popping up around the country. They help native-born Americans and immigrants interact and learn about each other's cultures.

SANCTUARY

The U.S. Constitution does not give the federal branch of government all the power. Some state, county, and city leaders who disagree with certain immigration policies and methods of enforcement have declared themselves sanctuary jurisdictions. These communities have passed laws to prevent their local police departments from putting individuals on an ICE detainer, also known as an immigration hold.

The March for Humanity in Philadelphia, 2017

credit: 7beachbum from Tsuruoka, Japan (CC BY 2.0)

According to the map on this site, what region of the country is most welcoming to immigrants? What factors could explain this?

Welcoming America network

IDENTITY NEWS

A detainer is a written request from ICE requesting local police to hold someone the police have under arrest for an additional 48 hours after the person is scheduled for release from jail. ICE wants this extra time to decide if it should take the individual into federal custody to begin deportation proceedings.

Compare the map of cities that have signed cooperation agreements with ICE to the map of sanctuary cities. Which has more? What factors might explain why some regions have many sanctuary cities and very few cooperating cities?

Cooperating cities

 city lab anti-sanctuary cities 2017

Sanctuary cities

 map sanctuary cities

The law does not require local police departments to keep people in custody just because ICE might want to deport them. Governors, mayors, and police chiefs of sanctuary jurisdictions believe that ICE detainers violate the Constitution. They believe people who have not been convicted of a crime or people who have served their sentences have the right to be released from custody.

In 2017, a spokesman for San Francisco mayor Ed Lee said, "If the federal government believes there is a need to detain a serious criminal, they can obtain a criminal warrant, which we will honor, as we always have . . . ."

The United States has a love-hate relationship with immigrants. Whether the nation will grow more welcoming or more hostile to newcomers in the future is uncertain, but one fact cannot be disputed: Millions of immigrants who live in the United States have already transformed the nation. They have transformed it socially, culturally, economically, and politically.

KEY QUESTIONS

- **What are some of the differences in immigration policy under Presidents Bush, Obama, and Trump?**

- **How does a government's policies toward immigrants influence the attitude of the citizens?**

- **Have you seen examples of discrimination in your community? How did it make you feel? How did you react?**

DECIPHER THE DRAWING

Political cartoonists pack a punch. They deliver opinions about issues such as immigration by exposing flaws in policies and the hypocrisy of political leaders. Analyzing political cartoons takes practice and an understanding of the techniques cartoonists use. How skilled are you at deciphering a political cartoonist's drawing?

- **Political cartoonists use the following techniques: metaphor, exaggeration, distortion, stereotype, labeling, analogy, and irony.** Look up the definitions of these words.

- **Can you spot any of these techniques in this nineteenth century anti-immigration cartoon?** The great fear of the period

- **Use the internet to locate pro- and anti-immigration cartoons about twenty-first century immigration.** Study the words, objects, and actions in the cartoons to determine what is happening. What images or symbols are used and what do they represent? Based on evidence from the cartoon and your knowledge about immigration in the United States, what is the artist's message?

> **To investigate more,** draw a political cartoon to communicate your opinion about some aspect of American immigration. You can even submit the cartoon to your school or town newspaper.

VOCAB LAB

Write down what you think each word means. What root words can you find to help you? What does the context of the word tell you?

Democrat, human trafficker, hypocrisy, Muslim, Republican, sanctuary city, and **zero tolerance.**

Compare your definitions with those of your friends or classmates. Did you all come up with the same meanings? Turn to the text and glossary if you need help.

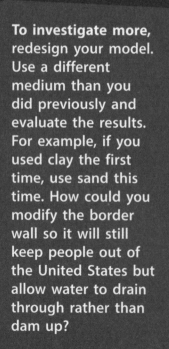

BORDER WALL OR RIVER DAM

A border wall across the Rio Grande Valley might reduce the number of undocumented immigrants entering the United States, but such a barrier could have devastating environmental consequences. The Rio Grande winds for 350 miles, much of it in a floodplain. The Southwest is known for unpredictable storms that can dump an inch or more of rain in minutes. The excess water runs into streams and creeks that rapidly overflow their banks. Design a model floodplain and investigate what impact a border wall could have during a flash flood.

- **Gather some materials to make a river running through a floodplain.** You will also be building a community of houses in the floodplain and a border wall.

- **Build your model floodplain community.**

  - Will your riverbed be wide, narrow, or average width?

  - How can you design your river so that the water runs "downstream"?

  - Where will you place your houses in the floodplain? How can you construct them?

- **Evaluate the impact of a flash flood on a river with no border wall inside it.** What happens when you dump several cups of water into your river quickly?

- **Install your wall in the middle of the river.** What happens this time when you dump a cup of water upstream in the river? What is different?

- **What can you conclude?** How will the installation of a border wall in low-lying areas of the Rio Grande affect communities that live near the river?

To investigate more, redesign your model. Use a different medium than you did previously and evaluate the results. For example, if you used clay the first time, use sand this time. How could you modify the border wall so it will still keep people out of the United States but allow water to drain through rather than dam up?

Chapter 5
America's Changing Face

BRUCE LEE SAID, "THE STIFFEST TREE IS THE MOST EASILY CRACKED, WHILE THE BAMBOO OR WILLOW SURVIVES BY BENDING WITH THE WIND."

How do immigrants shape the United States culturally and economically?

Immigration has transformed how the United States looks, tastes, and sounds. Immigrants have introduced music, language, food, and art that enrich the experience of living in this country.

In 2004, Tatsiana, a 22-year-old college student in Belarus, came to Wisconsin Dells, Wisconsin, on a short-term work visa. Back in Belarus, Tatsiana was studying economics, but in this small town that claims to be the waterpark capital of the world, she flipped burgers at a fast food restaurant. After a few days on the job, Tatsiana and a male coworker became friends. A summer of serving french fries and milkshakes side by side led to love, marriage, and eventually a green card for Tatsiana.

For a few years, Tatsiana worked a series of low-level jobs, confident these were "just stepping stones" to the life she wanted. In 2008, she began that life when she opened up a yoga studio. A decade later, the business is thriving. Tatsiana does not believe she could have had such success if she had remained in Belarus. In that country, she believes, government regulations there "choke you to death."

Tatsiana's story illustrates how immigrants shape the United States economically and culturally. Yoga, a physical and spiritual practice first introduced to nineteenth-century Americans by immigrants from India, is now being taught to Americans in the twenty-first century by an entrepreneurial immigrant from Belarus.

ECONOMIC IMPACTS OF IMMIGRATION

Immigration benefits the U.S. economy. Immigrants make up 13 percent of the U.S. population, and create 15 percent of the goods and services the country produces. More than 50 percent of America's billion-dollar companies were founded by immigrants, and each of these companies creates an average of 760 jobs.

Immigrants also pay a lot of taxes, far more than they use in public services. From 2002 to 2009, immigrants paid $115 billion more in Medicare taxes than they used in benefits. Economists project that between 2005 and 2080, immigrants will have contributed more than $600 billion to the Social Security system, money that will help keep the program afloat as aging Americans retire.[1]

While these numbers show that the overall effect of immigration is positive, some native-born workers do suffer financially when immigration is high. Wage trends show that a 10-percent increase in the number of workers in a certain field or in workers with particular skills results in a 3-percent decrease in wages. This wage drop hits the least-educated Americans hardest.

Immigrants and native-born Americans dominate different fields. While citizens tend to work in sales, business, finance, office support, and social services, immigrants are heavily employed in buildings and ground maintenance, construction, computers, math and science fields, and food prep and service occupations.

A professor of economics at Rutgers University analyzed economic data from 1940 to 2000. He found that when the number of low-skilled immigrants in society increased by 1 percent, the high school graduation rate of native-born Americans grew by 0.8 percent.

Here's what happens. The typical high school dropout earns $25,000 a year. In the last 20 years, immigrants without high school diplomas have increased the pool of unskilled workers by 25 percent. As a result, the earnings of poorly educated native-born American workers have dropped between $899 and $1,500 a year.[4] This decline does not mean lower wages per hour, but fewer jobs available or fewer hours worked.

This dark cloud, however, has a silver lining. When large numbers of low-skilled immigrants bring down the earnings of low-skilled native-born Americans, more Americans in general stay in school longer and look for better jobs.

Studies have shown that in the states with many immigrants, native-born American workers tended to leave low-skill jobs, such as those in fast food, and take jobs in fields such as customer service—jobs with higher wages that require communication skills.

First-generation immigrants do cost state and local governments a lot of money, but their children compensate for this.

Taxpayers foot a bill of about $50 billion a year in social services for new immigrants. Because immigrants from some parts of the world tend to have larger families than native-born Americans, most of this cost goes to educating immigrants' children. When these kids grow up, however, their labor produces a greater precentage of economic growth and tax revenue than does the work of native-born American workers. So in the long run, immigrants add money to the U.S. economy.

RACE AND ETHNICITY

The United States is changing color! In 1900, 90 percent of people living in America were European Americans, with the white skin and physical features that characterize people from that part of the world.

By 2000, this number had declined to 75 percent. Demographers predict that by the year 2045, people of European ancestry will no longer make up the majority of the U.S. population.

Since the Immigration and Nationality Act of 1965 brought immigrants to the United States from Africa and Asia, interracial marriages have led to an increased number of babies with brown skin. In states where Hispanic and Asian immigration is high—New Mexico, California, Texas, Washington, Oregon, Arizona, Nevada, and Colorado—one out of 10 marriages is between people of different races or ethnicities.

Through immigration, the population of the country has evolved into a colorful and cultural blend. In the 2000 census, 6.8 million people checked off more than one box to indicate their racial background. By 2010, that number had jumped by 32 percent.[6]

Identities are complex and even something to have fun with. Some people of African American and Mexican decent call themselves "Blaxican." On college campuses, young adults identify as "Filatino," "Chicanese," or "Korgentinian." Immigration pushes the country to rethink traditional notions of race and identity.

GLOBAL SNAPSHOT: BURKINI BAN

Lots of democracies, including the United States, prevent the government from favoring one religion over another. France goes further by prohibiting religious expression by private individuals in public places. As the number of Muslim immigrants in France has increased, the country has become embroiled in controversies about women's clothing. In 2004, the French government banned headscarves in schools. In 2010, it became illegal to wear the face-covering burqa in public. Then, in 2016, dozens of towns in France outlawed the burkini, the full-bodied swimsuit Muslim women wear to enjoy the beach while following their codes of modesty. France's highest court, however, outlawed the burkini ban, saying it interfered with "personal liberty." What do you think of clothing bans such as these?

LANGUAGE

In the spring of 2018, the video of a scene in a New York City deli went viral. When attorney Aaron Schlossberg witnessed customers ordering food in Spanish and the deli employees answering back in Spanish, he ranted at the restaurant's manager. "My guess is they're not documented," Aaron said in the video, "so my next call is to ICE to have each one of them kicked out of my country. . . . The least they can do is speak English."

No one is required to speak English in the United States, although people have tried to make this the law. Since 2003, eight bills have been introduced in Congress to make English the official language of the United States, but each bill failed to pass.

When immigrants from Great Britain settled North America in the 1600s, the English language took root. But diversity made this a land of many tongues. Native American tribes and enslaved Africans spoke their own languages. By 1783, one-quarter of the population was speaking in Dutch, French, or German. According to the 1910 census, 10 million American immigrants spoke a main language that was not English.

A sign for sale in a store in 2009

credit: CGP Grey (CC BY 2.0)

When the National Origins Act of 1924 slashed immigration, the variety of languages spoken on America's streets declined. After 1965, when immigration revived again, so did rich linguistic diversity. The Census Department estimates that people living in America today speak more than 300 languages.

The English language is not under threat in the United States. Most of the population speaks it, and English remains the language of business, government, and law.

> Rather than English dying out due to immigration, the opposite is true.

The United States is a graveyard for immigrant languages. Only one-third of the children of immigrants speak their parents' native tongue well by the time they reach adulthood. This number drops to 12 percent by the third generation of immigrants.

MUSIC

American music was composed by immigrants. Not only did they bring their sounds and rhythms with them to the United States, but they also applied their skills and experience to their new environment to create distinct sounds. The world has immigrants to thank for jazz, blues, gospel, ragtime, and show tunes.

The immigrant's stamp on American music goes back centuries. In 1804, New Orleans, Louisiana, became part of the United States. With it came an explosion of sound utterly unlike the music of white European culture centered on the East Coast.

ONLY ENGLISH SPOKEN HERE

The United States has long tried to force people to speak only English. Enslaved Africans were forbidden to speak their own languages because owners feared they could plot rebellions without being detected. During the early twentieth century, Native American children forced to attend government boarding schools were punished when they did not speak English. German was dropped from school curriculums when the United States went to war with Germany during World War I. And Japanese schools started by immigrants in Hawaii were shut down after the United States declared war on Japan in 1941. What language do you speak at home? Why is language such an important part of a people's identity?

Enslaved people were allowed to gather occasionally in Congo Square, an open market in New Orleans. Here, they played the music of their homelands in Africa. To the beat of a drummer pounding on a barrel, men and women danced so rhythmically and for so long that spectators compared them to machines. After the Civil War, the music from formerly enslaved Africans evolved into blues, gospel, and jazz.

The compositions of Irving Berlin (1888–1989)—born Israel Beilin—are an example of the impact that European Jewish immigrants had on Broadway and Hollywood. Irving emigrated from Russia with his family in 1893 when he was five. Waves of anti-Semitic violence frequently cascaded through Europe, and when someone burned down their home, the Beilins decided to start a new life in America. The family of eight settled in a three-room tenement on New York City's Lower East Side. The only place Irving could get fresh air was on the fire escape or the roof.

When Irving was eight, his father died. The boy dropped out of school and earned pennies as a street singer outside clubs. Later, he found work as a singing waiter and wrote songs in his spare time.

Listen to the music of California immigration on this website. What do you think the role of traditional music is for immigrants when they enter a new country?

California migration music

A New Orleans street band

credit: Infrogmation of New Orleans (CC BY 2.0)

Irving's first major hit came in 1911 with "Alexander's Ragtime Band." In a career that spanned more than 50 years, Irving's music rallied the troops during two world wars. His songs, such as "White Christmas" and "God Bless America," became part of the fabric of American life in the twentieth century.

Latin rhythms showed up in the music of the United States in the twentieth century with immigrants from the Caribbean. By the 1950s, Cuban, Puerto Rican, and Dominican immigrants to New York City had infused Latin rhythms into new American musical styles such as mambo, rumba, merengue, salsa, and Latin jazz. At the end of the twentieth century, Latino musicians helped form the new genres of hip-hop and reggaeton.

Irving Berlin playing piano with the stars of the film, *Alexander's Ragtime Band*

FOOD

Every country has food typical to its culture. Pelmini are Russian ravioli. Sadza is a cornmeal stew made in Zimbabwe. Buñuelos are fried doughnuts from Mexico.

What food symbolizes uniquely American cuisine?

Hamburgers? Thank German immigrants for the ground meat patty. Pizza? Italian immigrants brought this flat bread to the United States in the late nineteenth century. Tacos? They came across the southern border from Mexico.

Just like music, the foods different ethnic groups prepared have evolved in the new American environment. Some traditional ingredients could not be easily found in the United States, so local substitutes were used instead.

Hear the sounds of different percussion instruments Latin American and Caribbean immigrants introduced into American music.

 A Different Drum LOC

Also, when different ethnic groups live closely in crowded cities, they learn from each other and recipes are transformed. Pizza is the perfect example. In the early 1800s, Naples was a busy, waterfront city in southern Italy. Poor dockworkers gobbled cheap, easy-to-eat pizzas sold by street vendors. The flatbreads were topped with local tomatoes, garlic, anchovies, and olive oil.

When immigrants from Naples came to the United States in the late nineteenth and early twentieth centuries, they cooked pizza in ovens in New York, Boston, Chicago, and other cities. As Italian immigrants moved to the suburbs, pizza moved, too. After World War II, American soldiers returned home from fighting in Italy with a taste for pizza, and the food began to be consumed by non-Italians.

By the 1950s, pizza was no longer considered an ethnic dish, and toppings were no longer limited to what the Neapolitans had put on flatbread. In the twenty-first century, gourmet pizzas can be topped with anything from mashed potatoes to pineapple to kielbasa to hummus. Pizza has become American.

As seamlessly as immigrant traditions have been woven into the American identity, both scholars and political leaders would insist that the United States' current immigration system must be reformed. Whether such reform is possible, given the current deep political divide in the United States, is the topic of the next chapter.

WHAT'S COOKING?

Which of these immigrant foods is your favorite?

- Irish: corned beef and cabbage
- German: hotdogs, hamburgers, sauerkraut
- European Jewish: kosher pickles, bagels
- Mexican: tacos and salsa
- Chinese: fried rice, egg rolls
- Japanese: sushi
- Middle Eastern: shish kebab

KEY QUESTIONS

- **How have different ethnicities affected your daily life in terms of food, music, language, and entertainment?**
- **Should society work to preserve different traditions and languages? Why or why not?**

CELEBRATE AMERICA'S CULINARY HISTORY WITH AN IMMIGRANT POTLUCK

What does the United States' immigration heritage taste like? Team up with several peers or classmates to prepare some dishes from around the world. Savor the flavor immigrants have added to the nation's cuisine.

- **Locate a cookbook that features recipes from immigrants to the United States.** You can also use *The Great American Potluck*, which is recipes collected by the Library of Congress from immigrants between 2002 and 2006.

 Great American potluck

- **Divide up recipes so all global regions are represented.**

- **Prepare a menu for your feast.** Inform your guests of the origin of each dish they are eating and explain the meal's connection to immigration.

- **Invite parents or community members to your immigrant potluck.**

To investigate more, explore what happens to the diet of immigrants after they move to the United States. Several studies suggest that the longer immigrants live in the United States, the worse their health becomes. Why do you think becoming an American could be hazardous to an immigrant's health?

VOCAB LAB

Write down what you think each word means. What root words can you find to help you? What does the context of the word tell you?

anti-Semitic, **burkini**, **burqa**, **culture**, **diversity**, **heritage**, **identity**, **interracial**, and **linguistic**.

Compare your definitions with those of your friends or classmates. Did you all come up with the same meanings? Turn to the text and glossary if you need help.

WHAT'S ON YOUR PLATE?

Very few Americans grow their own vegetables, milk their own cows, or butcher their own meat. We go to the grocery store, where almost any food is available any season of the year. Have you ever considered the lives of the people whose labor brings that food to your plate?

A 2014 report by the American Farm Bureau Federation found the agricultural industry needs between 1.5 and 2 million workers. Because not enough legal immigrants or American citizens will do backbreaking farm labor, 50 to 70 percent of agricultural workers are undocumented immigrants.[8]

Explore the relationship between immigrant labor and the foods you eat often. How much do you rely on farm workers?

- **Keep a food diary for one week.** What fresh fruit, fresh vegetables, milk, and meat do you regularly consume?

- **Select one of these foods and research the role undocumented immigrants play in getting that item from the farm or field to the grocery store.** What do immigrants say about their work experiences in places such as chicken processing plants or California vineyards? What makes the work difficult? What do they get paid for their work and how do their wages impact the price you pay at the grocery store?

- **In a creative way, communicate the journey this food took.** Consider a short story, comic strip, or storyboard. Share the story with your classmates and discuss how Americans benefit from the labor of undocumented immigrants.

> **To investigate more,** change your story so all the workers who produced your food were paid minimum wage. What impact would this have on you as a consumer?

Chapter 6 ▶

Immigration Reform

Why can't lawmakers and citizens agree on a path forward for immigration policy reform?

A political divide is stalling immigration reform, as people and politicians act out of personal bias, fear, and economic concerns. Finding common ground seems to be getting more difficult as America becomes home to more immigrants.

On January 30, 2018, President Trump stood before a joint session of Congress to deliver his first "State of the Union" speech. The audience of lawmakers, Supreme Court justices, and honored guests clapped often. But when President Trump began to discuss immigration, the mood changed.

The president described the immigration system as "broken," and Republicans clapped while Democrats scowled. When Trump urged Congress to fund his southern border wall, Republicans stood. Democrats remained seated. Trump called for an end to "chain migration." Republicans cheered, but Democrats booed.

These political divisions illustrate why efforts to reform the immigration system in the twenty-first century have failed.

THE TURNING POINT

The political divide that is crippling immigration reform began with nationwide protests in the spring of 2006. On March 10, more than 100,000 people flooded downtown Chicago, Illinois. Cries of "Si, se puede" (Yes, we can), ricocheted off skyscrapers. Similar rallies occurred in more than 140 cities in 39 states as immigrants and their allies spoke out against a bill being debated in the Senate. The bill would have made it illegal for anyone to provide food, housing, or medical aid to undocumented immigrants.

The protests culminated on May 1, when immigrants went on a one-day strike. One of the rallying cries during the protests was, "Today, we march, tomorrow, we vote!" In that year's midterm election, Latinos abandoned Republican candidates, the party that backed the bill. Politicians paid attention, and the bill failed in Congress.

The protests ended, but they sparked a conservative backlash. When undocumented immigrants remained in the shadows picking crops, busing tables, and digging ditches, the debate about immigration was limited to border communities. The massive demonstrations sparked conversations about immigration in America's heartland and some people responded radically.

Armed vigilante groups such as the Minute Men established outposts on the southern border. Sporting badges labeled "Undocumented Border Patrol Agent," these men patrolled for undocumented immigrants sneaking into the country. State legislators in Arizona, Georgia, and Indiana passed tough laws that targeted undocumented immigrants, and politicians who campaigned for tighter border restrictions were elected to Congress.

IDENTITY NEWS

Conservative radio hosts raised false alarms about undocumented immigrants bringing crime and diseases, including drug-resistant tuberculosis, to the United States.

This swing to the right on immigration made future reform efforts even more fraught. In 2007, Republican President George W. Bush crafted a compromise that would have created a path to legalization for undocumented immigrants in the country in exchange for stricter border security. But newly elected Republican members of Congress refused to grant amnesty to the undocumented. Some pro-labor Democrats also opposed the plan because they feared immigrant workers would take American jobs. The bill died in the Senate.

The next year, immigration advocates pressured Democratic President Barack Obama to fulfill his campaign pledge, so he urged Congress to pass a comprehensive reform bill. But Obama had used much of his political clout in his fight to pass a health care bill that every single Republican member of Congress opposed.

A peaceful demonstration in 2010

credit: Arasmus Photo (CC BY 2.0)

Feelings on all sides were bruised and few lawmakers wanted to compromise with the opposing party. Then, in the midterm election of 2010, conservative Republicans won control of the House of Representatives. Immigration reform was no longer part of conversations in Washington, DC.

Reformers' hopes rose again in 2013, when the "Gang of Eight," four Democrat and four Republican senators, crafted a compromise immigration reform bill. But a bill cannot become a law unless it wins the support of both houses of Congress. The House of Representatives refused to consider the Senate's bill. Reform fell apart again.

IDEOLOGICAL DIFFERENCES

The platforms of the Democratic and Republican parties in the 2016 election show their different goals for immigration reform.

Each failed immigration reform effort has spotlighted the ideological divide between Republicans and Democrats on immigration, a gap that seems impossible to cross.

What Republicans Want	What Democrats Want
Wall off the 2,000-mile border with Mexico	Provide a path to citizenship for law-abiding, undocumented immigrants
Give special scrutiny to immigrants from countries associated with Islamic terrorism	Work to address the root causes of violence in Central America that prompt people to emigrate
Photograph and fingerprint male immigrants from 25 mainly Muslim countries	Expand the use of temporary protected status
Reduce legal immigration	Provide government-funded counseling for unaccompanied minors in deportation proceedings
Revise criteria for granting people asylum and refugee status	End raids and roundups of families

DREAMS DEFERRED

Democrat and Republican lawmakers agree on one group of immigrants they must help—the Dreamers. These are the undocumented young people whose parents brought them to the United States as children. Many came as infants and toddlers. America is the only country they have ever known. Without legal status, the Dreamers face a crippling future.

As their high school peers graduate high school and go on to college, these youth cannot get a driver's license, financial aid, or a work permit.

Efforts to aid these young people began back in 2001 when the Development, Relief, and Education for Alien Minors (DREAM) Act was first introduced in Congress. This bill would have allowed undocumented young people a pathway to United States citizenship through college, work, or the military.

The DREAM Act almost became law more than once. In 2007, the bill fell seven votes short in the Senate. Three years later, a revised DREAM Act passed the House of Representatives, but, as 200 Dreamers watched from the gallery, the bill again failed to pass the Senate.

Frustrated and afraid, Dreamers turned to their president for help. Young Latinos, many ineligible to vote, had campaigned for Barack Obama in 2008. Their efforts helped Obama win 71 percent of Latino votes and the election. It was payback time. Dreamers wanted Obama to use his executive power to help them.

TRAIL OF DREAMS

On January 1, 2010, four college students set off on a 1,500-mile march from Miami, Florida, to Washington, DC, to draw attention to the plight of undocumented young people. Juan Rodriguez, Carlos Roa, Gaby Pacheco, and Felipe Matos met on the campus of Miami-Dade College. The friends demonstrated against the detention of classmates and friends, but when authorities ignored these protests, they decided to take their action on the road. Every day from 8 a.m. to 6 p.m., they walked. At night, they slept in a donated RV. Along the way, the students stopped in communities to tell their stories of life in the shadows. They reached the Capitol on May 1, 2010.

Obama was gearing up to run for reelection in 2012. He would need Latino votes again, but that community was unhappy with him. Immigrant rights supporters called Obama the "deporter in chief" because of the large number of undocumented immigrants deported under his administration. In an interview with Univision, an American Spanish language network, Obama insisted that immigration officials were deporting criminals. "We aren't going around rounding up students," he said. "That is completely false."[1]

A few days later, when the president was speaking at a Latino town hall meeting, a young woman told the president how ICE had arrested and jailed her. She held up her deportation order and demanded to know why, if ICE was not deporting college students, Dreamers such as her were being kicked out of the country.

The president grew defensive. America was a nation of laws, and as president he had to enforce them. "I don't have a choice about that," Obama said. "That's part of my job."[2] This was not the answer Dreamers were looking for.

During a speech in July 2011, Obama was interrupted by hecklers when he claimed he could not bypass Congress to help the Dreamers. "Yes, you can!" they chanted. The phrase had been Obama's 2008 campaign slogan. In 2012, Dreamers occupied Obama's campaign office in Denver, Colorado.

Obama eventually responded to the Dreamers' demands. In the spring of 2012, the president signed the executive order Deferred Action for Childhood Arrivals, or DACA. Although Obama had said he could not bypass Congress, with this executive order he did just that.

GLOBAL SNAPSHOT: ITALY SHUTS ITS DOOR

The United States is not the only country closing its doors to migrants. Asylum seekers from Africa and the Middle East often try to cross the Mediterranean Sea on flimsy rubber dinghies. When the migrant crisis began in 2013, Italy led the rescue of drowning migrants. But the Italian public grew weary of the influx of foreigners and elected a conservative government in 2018. In June 2018, this new government refused to allow a rescue ship to dock in an Italian port, a ship that carried 629 migrants, including children, pregnant women, and wounded passengers. Spain eventually accepted the vessel. The incident shows the strain the migrant crisis is taking on relationships between countries in the European Union.

HOPE DIES LAST

From Thanksgiving 2017 until the vote on an immigration reform bill was held in the second week of February 2018, DACA recipients from across the country peacefully protested Congress. Dreamers were a constant presence in the hallways, offices, and elevators of the Capitol Building. Polite but persistent, these immigrants questioned their lawmakers and shared their experiences of life in legal limbo. José Patiño, a DACA recipient and immigration activist, said Dreamers had to keep their hopes up because, "ultimately, that's all we have."

DACA gave special protection to undocumented immigrants who were less than 30 years old and who had immigrated to the United States before their 16th birthday. Immigrants in this age group must have lived continuously in the United States for at least five years and be enrolled in college, in the military, or employed. DACA granted these immigrants two years of legal residency. This was not the equivalent of a green card, but it transformed the lives of Dreamers.

Julio Salgado said the most important change for him was getting a driver's license. The ability to drive gave him "a sense of freedom."[3]

> However, his joy was tinged with grief. His parents did not qualify for DACA and had no protection from deportation.

President Trump speaks at U.S. Central Command and U.S. Special Operations Command at MacDill, 2017

credit: Chairman of the Joint Chiefs of Staff from Washington D.C, United States

When President Obama signed DACA on June 12, 2012, he called it a "temporary stopgap measure." Executive orders can be undone by the next president. And that is exactly what happened when Donald Trump took office in 2016.

On September 5, 2017, Attorney General Jeff Sessions stood in front of a room full of reporters at the Justice Department and announced DACA would end the following spring. President Trump called DACA an "amnesty-first approach,"[5] and said if Congress wanted Dreamers to have legal status, lawmakers must pass a law before DACA expired.

The Senate took up Trump's challenge on February 12, 2018. Lawmakers tried to craft an immigration reform bill from different proposals. One plan, supported by President Trump and put forward by Republican Senator Chuck Grassley, would have legalized 1.8 million undocumented young immigrants, spent $25 billion on border security, slashed family-based immigration, and ended the diversity lottery.

The proposal that had the most support was a plan created by a bipartisan group of senators who called themselves the "Common Sense Caucus." Their plan had key similarities to the Grassley plan. It would have legalized the same immigrants as Senator Grassley's plan and put the same amount of money into border security. The Common Sense Caucus also wanted to reduce family immigration, but not as severely as the Grassley plan, and would keep the diversity lottery.

Neither bill received enough votes to get out of the Senate. On February 15, 2018, Senate Majority Leader Mitch McConnell (1942–) said, "I think it's safe to say this has been a disappointing week."[6]

Attorney General Sessions criticized President Obama for using the power of the executive branch to take action that lawmakers had repeatedly refused to do. He called this an "unconstitutional exercise of authority by the executive branch" and claimed that DACA denied jobs to "hundreds of thousands of Americans by allowing . . . illegal aliens to take those jobs."[4]

A rally in support of DACA in 2017

credit: Molly Adams (CC BY 2.0)

COURT FIGHT

The Dreamers are not the only ones using the courts as a tool in the struggle to reform immigration. Their opponents are, too. In May 2018, the attorneys-general from seven states whose governors oppose DACA sued the Trump administration. They want DACA terminated immediately instead of phased out, as the president plans to do.

The courts offered some breathing room for Dreamers. As soon as the Trump administration announced DACA was ending, immigrant-rights groups filed suits. In January 2018, a federal district court ordered the Trump administration to keep accepting renewal applications from people already enrolled in DACA while the lawsuits work their way through the courts.

The legal process is not fast. DACA is likely to wind up on the docket of the Supreme Court of the United States, but no one knows when. Meanwhile, Dreamers live in limbo, uncertain of what the future may bring.

FEAR OF CHANGE

According to a Pew Research Center poll conducted in June 2018, 73 percent of Americans support granting permanent legal status to Dreamers. The same poll found that a majority of Americans want current levels of legal immigration to either stay the same or rise. If this poll data is accurate, why is it so difficult to reform immigration law? The answer lies in politics, sociology, and psychology.

Politically, the country is fragmented. Lawmakers from both parties have gerrymandered the electoral maps of their states. They have changed the boundaries of their congressional districts to favor one party over the other. This means a congressperson often represents a district with voters that mostly support one political party. There is no incentive to compromise because their voters back home do not demand it.

Sociology—the way people relate in groups—also gets in the way of immigration reform. Research shows that voters do not know much about immigration policy. Instead, they vote for leaders based on traits such as race, religion, and class. Once voters define themselves as Democrats or Republicans, they believe whatever the party tells them about an issue. According to this theory, the will of the people does not shape the immigration policies of the Democratic or Republican Parties. Rather, the political parties we identify with tell us what to believe about immigration. But what the parties tell voters is not always based on fact.

The psychology, or mindset, of people affects how they vote and how willing they are to compromise on controversial issues such as immigration. Many Americans hold deep racial and ethnic prejudices that are hard to uproot.

In one study, researchers questioned white Americans' attitudes about undocumented German, Chinese, and Mexican immigrants. The respondents rated the Mexican immigrants lower than the Chinese and Germans because they assumed the Mexican immigrants were uneducated and would refuse to adapt to American culture. Respondents had not been given any information about the immigrants other than their undocumented status and ethnicities. The respondents' bias filled in the missing gaps.

Take a look at how, depending on how political districts are drawn, an election can be decided different ways. The total number of votes for pink and green doesn't change, but the district boundaries do, resulting in different outcomes.

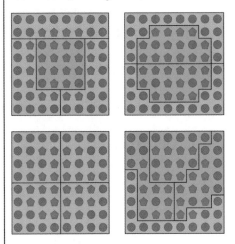

The Southern Poverty Law Center tracks the number and location of hate groups in the United States. Go to the group's website to view a map of these groups. What type of hate organizations exist in your state? Why do some areas of the country have more active hate groups than other areas? What are the differences in the beliefs of these groups?

SPLC hate map

KEY QUESTIONS

- **Can you think of some solutions to the problem of gerrymandering?**

- **How can those people who are creating immigration policies work to keep their personal biases in check?**

- **How might society change when white people are no longer the majority population?**

Ethnocentrism and racism are forms of bias.

When people judge another culture based on the values and standards of their own culture, they are being ethnocentric. If you grow up in the United States, where public restrooms are free, and you travel to Poland, where you discover you have to pay an attendant 50 cents to enter a public restroom, you might think such a custom is stupid. That is ethnocentrism.

Racism is a kind of biological ethnocentrism. Racist people believe that groups that share certain physical traits, such as skin color, hair texture, and facial features, are naturally superior to others.

The future of a majority nonwhite United States is still a ways off. However, in 2013, one study found that the average person believed 49 percent—almost half—of the people who lived in the United States were not white. In reality, the number was 37 percent.[7]

This is the moment in American history when many in the majority culture—white people whose ancestors came from Europe—feel the United States no longer looks or thinks like them. Numerous studies have shown that when white voters are given evidence that the country is becoming more racially and ethnically diverse, they support more conservative policies, including immigration restrictions.

As the twenty-first century progresses, America will grow increasingly diverse as immigrants move here via different methods. How will this affect immigration reform and the evolving American identity? The final chapter of this book explores the future of immigration in the United States.

LOGICAL FALLACIES

Constructive debate is essential to effectively reforming the U.S. immigration system. However, too often people use logical fallacies when they argue. A logical fallacy is an error in thinking that makes an entire argument invalid. It is important to recognize fallacies in the arguments of both other people and yourself.

- **Use the internet to research the following types of fallacies:**

  - Ad hominem
  - Straw man
  - Red herring
  - Appeal to ignorance
  - False dilemma/ false dichotomy

  - Slippery slope
  - Circular argument
  - Hasty generalization
  - Tu quoque/appeal to hypocrisy
  - Causal fallacy

- **Below are some logical fallacies about immigration.** Try to identify the type of error each statement represents.

  - If DACA recipients are given a path to citizenship, Mexican immigrants will come flooding over the border.
  - Immigrants pay tribute to the greatness of our country by wanting to come here. Therefore, the annual number of immigrants should be increased.
  - The United States cannot pass immigration reform until it secures the border.
  - After the huge wave of immigration at the turn of the twentieth century, America went on to greatness. Therefore, immigration is good for the country.

VOCAB LAB

Write down what you think each word means. What root words can you find to help you? What does the context of the word tell you?

bias, **compromise**, **controversial**, **ethnocentrism**, **gerrymander**, **influx**, **logical fallacy**, and **vigilante**.

Compare your definitions with those of your friends or classmates. Did you all come up with the same meanings? Turn to the text and glossary if you need help.

To investigate more, imagine you are engaged in a debate with someone and they make some of these statements. How would you respond?

CIVIC ACTION

Although you cannot vote in the United States until you reach age 18, you can speak out. In 2018, students from Marjory Stoneman Douglas High School coordinated nationwide walkouts to protest gun violence. In 2014, young people marched with the Black Lives Matter movement to protest police shootings of African American men. What action will you take about an issue you care about?

- **Identify issues important to you and your community.** Select one issue you want to act on.

- **Research the issue.** What improvements would you like to see?

- **What is your goal?** What person or group in society has the power to make this goal a reality?

- **Develop a plan for how you can communicate your vision with the person or group in power.** Will your plan involve letters, meetings with policymakers, proposals, or activities?

- **Carry out your action plan.**

- **Reflect on your effort.** What were your successes and challenges? What lessons did you learn to improve your activism strategies in the future?

To investigate more, explore times in the twentieth century when young people participated in social movements to reform the nation. Consider the March of the Mill Children in 1903, the Little Rock Nine in 1957, the Children's Crusade of 1963, *Tinker v. Des Moines* in 1969, the Chicano Blowouts of 1968, and the Old Enough to Vote marches of 1971.

What impact did these movements have? What strategies did the young activists have in common? What determined the success or failure of each action?

Chapter 7 ▶
Out of Many, One

What does the future hold for today's immigrants?

Many of today's immigrants will become tomorrow's Americans. Immigrants do assimilate. But because the process is slow, it is not always visible.

On February 16, 2017, immigrants across the country went on strike. They did not go to work or shop. They did not fill up their vehicles with gas or go to a movie. This Day Without Immigrants was an act of civil disobedience to demonstrate how important immigrants are to the U.S. economy.

In Charlotte, North Carolina, classrooms were half empty. In Milwaukee, Wisconsin, thousands of protesters marched to the county courthouse chanting, "The people united will never be defeated." Matt Carr, owner of a Washington, DC, restaurant, supported his striking employees. "Without them," he said, "our small businesses would crumble."[1]

How much this strike hurt the nation's wallet is hard to calculate, but experts agree that immigrants are vital to the economy.

Daniel Costa, who was director of immigration law and policy research at the Economic Policy Institute, said, "If all immigrants were just to disappear from the U.S. workforce tomorrow . . . you'd feel an impact and loss in . . . many different occupations and industries, from construction and landscape to finance and information technology."

An America without immigrants is an unlikely scenario, but the Trump administration does want to severely cut immigration, both undocumented and legal. What would such a future America look like?

MAKING AMERICA WHITE AGAIN

President Trump has said that he wants to reduce legal immigration by half by 2028. He would achieve this by restricting the number of family members sponsored by citizens and permanent residents and by eliminating the diversity lottery.

Fewer immigrants means fewer workers producing goods and services. According to an analysis by *The Washington Post*, under Trump's plan, the U.S. economy could shrink by as much as $1 trillion during the next 20 years.

The absence of young immigrant workers would also endanger the safety net for elderly Americans. Four out of every five immigrants predicted to come to the United States during the next few decades are under 40 years old. And 50 percent of Americans are over that age. As older Americans retire, they will depend on Social Security and Medicare. Without enough young workers paying taxes, these programs could go bankrupt.

IDENTITY NEWS

Americans who like to eat out or vacation might find services lacking if cuts are made to immigration. Immigrants account for 31 percent of hotel workers, 22 percent of food service workers, 43 percent of owners of small hotels and motels, and 37 percent of small restaurant owners.[2]

With such a gloomy economic forecast, why does the Trump administration want to reduce immigration so drastically? Some analysts believe this is an effort to slow down the racial changes happening in the country. The Census Bureau projected that with the current immigration system, by 2044, minority groups will outnumber non-Hispanic whites in the United States. Could Trump's policies be designed to stall this change?

> If President Trump's plan became law, it would not alter the country's fundamental path.

The future of America's identity still trends away from white. From 2010 to 2016, the native-born Hispanic population grew by 5 million people. During that same time, the native-born white population shrank by 400,000. According to Roberto Suro, an immigration expert at the University of Southern California, "If your primary concern is that the American population is becoming less white, it's already too late."

President Trump's immigration plan is unlikely to become law. Many Democrats and moderate Republicans believe the plan slashes immigration too deeply. Few politicians mention another option for America's future because they think it is more radical than even the president's proposal—open borders.

LOSING IMMIGRANTS

Slashing legal immigration by half would close the door to about 20 million immigrants for the next 40 years. The cap on family migration would sharply reduce the number of Asian immigrants. And the end of the diversity lottery would affect people from Africa and the Caribbean the most.

OPEN BORDERS

How would the world be different if people were free to move wherever they wanted to find work? That's what open borders mean. If immigration laws disappeared, the United States would look very different in the future.

Most politicians avoid talking about open borders because the concept is very controversial, but scholars debate the topic. Experts who support open borders believe that eliminating immigration restrictions would reduce global poverty. Development economist Michael Clemens argues that if developed countries reduced barriers to immigration, the gross domestic product (GDP) of the world would double.

Open borders could reduce poverty because human labor is valuable and immigration regulations waste lots of human labor. People who live in poor countries are less productive because of problems such as war, corruption, poor roads and bridges, and lack of technology. These problems make finding work and getting to and from work challenging.

When workers move from a poor country to a rich one, they become more productive. For example, a worker at a shoe factory in Afghanistan might move material with a push cart and use hand tools. When that worker moves to Great Britain, he uses a forklift to move pallets of materials and assembles shoes with power tools.

More productivity increases the wealth of the economy and the worker. Mexican laborers who move to the United States earn on average 150 percent more money than they did in Mexico, and Nigerian laborers make up to 1,000 percent more.[3]

Critics of open borders worry that letting foreigners move to the United States to work will cost Americans their jobs. Experts call that line of thinking the "lump of labor fallacy." It relies on the belief that the United States has a fixed number of jobs, and only that number is available to be divided up. In reality, when immigrants enter the country, their labor creates brand new jobs.

IDENTITY NEWS

Many people who live in Mexico cross the border every day to jobs in the United States. The busiest crossing point is between Tijuana, Mexico, and San Diego, California. An estimated 120,000 commuters, 6,000 trucks, and 63,000 pedestrians cross daily. A 2013 study by the U.S. Department of Agriculture estimated the cost of wait times to cross the U.S.-Mexican border is $12 billion a year in wasted productivity.

Say you own a restaurant in Madison, Wisconsin, and employ six workers. When immigrants move into the neighborhood, they dine at your restaurant and business picks up so much that your six employees need help. You hire three more workers, two of whom are immigrants. You have just created three new jobs. Also, your new employees spend their wages to shop at neighborhood stores. Business also picks up at these stores and the stores need to hire more workers.

Despite evidence that open borders would reduce global poverty, 79 percent of Americans believe the nation needs "secure borders." People worry about the effects of large-scale immigration. But many of these worries are based more on myth than fact.

Economist Bryan Caplan at George Mason University has suggested "keyhole" solutions to address the public fears about large-scale immigration. A keyhole solution targets specific problems through focused solutions rather than restricting an entire activity. For example, if evidence proves that many immigrants do not learn how to speak English, then charge them a special tax until they pass an English competency test. Keyhole solutions have the potential to calm the fears of Americans who are uncomfortable with rapid cultural change.

An immigrant rights March in 2006

credit: Jonathan McIntosh (CC BY 2.5)

BECOMING AMERICAN

Some experts believe Americans do not fear immigration, but the lack of assimilation. Immigrants do not strip off their culture and button on a new one as if they were putting on a shirt. Assimilation takes years, even a lifetime.

Javier, the boy you met in Chapter 1 who emigrated from Mexico when he was 12, has learned "to accept the United States as my adopted nation." Occasionally, he still feels like a stranger in a strange land. At times, these feelings are sparked by someone asking, "Are you legal?"

> Javier said the hardest part of being an immigrant "is finding the strength to just fit in."

But after 22 years of living in the United States, Javier has successfully adapted. He married a Caucasian woman and they are raising their daughter to be proud of her Mexican-American heritage. He has applied for naturalization and is preparing for his citizenship test.

Native-born Americans may not understand how the process of assimilation works. They want it to be quick. A 2017 Pew survey found that only 50 percent of respondents believed a person had to be born in the United States to be considered an American, but 90 percent said a person could not be "truly American" unless they spoke English. And 85 percent believed it was important to "share American customs and traditions." Immigrants do assimilate, but because the process is slow, it is not always visible.

GENERATIONS

In May 2018, White House Chief of Staff John Kelly described Central American immigrants as "overwhelmingly rural people . . . . They don't speak English . . . . They don't integrate well; they don't have skills."[4] According to research by the Cato Institute, the Central American immigrants that have arrived in the United States in the twenty-first century assimilate as well as John Kelly's ancestors did when they arrived in the twentieth century. The chief of staff's great-grandmother emigrated from Italy, lived in the United States for 30 years, and never learned English. But John Kelly is certainly an American. That is because assimilation takes generations.

Immigrants and their children integrate into American society more easily than into European society. The United States has more entry-level jobs for immigrants, whereas one-fifth of immigrants in the European Union are unemployed. The children of immigrants in Europe have a 50-percent unemployment rate. In the United States, second-generation immigrants are employed at the same rate as native-born Americans. Children of immigrants born in the United States automatically become U.S. citizens, but this is not true in most European countries.[5]

Assimilation falls into three different categories—economic, cultural, and civic. The experiences of some of the immigrants you met in earlier chapters illustrate the assimilation process.

Tatsiana, the woman from Belarus, has partially assimilated after 14 years in the United States. She and her husband are successful small business owners and own a home, both signs of economic assimilation.

Cultural integration is happening more slowly for Tatsiana, especially in fashion and food. In Belarus, a woman would not leave the house without paying careful attention to her makeup and clothes. Tatsiana was shocked when she saw American women shopping in pajama pants! In Belarus, everything her family cooked was made with fresh ingredients, while in the States, food can come from a box or a drive-through lane. Tatsiana has not shed all Belarusian customs, but admits that occasionally she goes shopping in sweats and sometimes cooks a box of macaroni and cheese for her daughter.

Civic engagement is more complicated for Tatsiana. She is not a citizen and cannot vote. Although she does not plan to live in Belarus again, she returns regularly to see her family. If she became an American citizen, she would have to give up her Belarus citizenship, which would make visiting her family much more complicated.

Tatsiana still calls herself a Belarusian, but recognizes her lifestyle is becoming more American. She's happy with that. "Honestly," she said, "I feel honored that America has accepted me." Tatsiana does not feel vulnerable without American citizenship.

She recognizes that her European heritage and white skin give her a degree of protection some immigrants do not have.

B.P., the man who emigrated from St. Lucia, found both his dark skin and immigrant status obstacles to assimilation. Employees have trailed him in stores, customers have told him to "go back to your country," and police have stopped him without cause.

An incident at an airport pushed B.P. to get his U.S. citizenship. On a return trip from St. Lucia, customs agents interrogated B.P. for hours. "You don't have any rights," an agent told him. "I can do anything I want and you can't do anything about it."

B.P. knew then he needed to become a citizen to protect himself. The process was difficult and required a lawyer's help. But now, B.P. sees himself as an American. He votes in every election and campaigns for candidates he supports.

IDENTITY NEWS

Race relations are one part of American culture that B.P. refuses to accept. As a black man, he lives with constant anxiety. "Every day I'm afraid I won't return to my family," B.P. said. "I'm afraid I might get shot."

St. Lucia, the home B.P. left behind to come to America

St. Lucia, however, remains B.P.'s cultural home. He hopes to return to live on the island some day with his wife and children. "That's where my roots are," he said. "I feel so free when I can speak the language of my people. I just love that feeling."

Civic engagement drew Pastor Procopio to apply for U.S. citizenship. He realized that government policies and laws could grant rights and benefits to the undocumented immigrants who make up his congregation. After Procopio became a citizen in 2017, he intended to use his new powers: "My vote can change history."

Procopio had great faith in America and felt welcomed by its embrace. But then, in the summer of 2018, immigration officials denied a green card to his wife, Cristina, charging that she "illegally smuggled" her children into the United States. Procopio and Cristina's oldest two children emigrated on their own as adults without documentation, and Cristina and the younger two children followed two years later. What Cristina and Procopio consider an act of love to reunite their family, ICE labels "smuggling." Cristina was deported and barred from reentering the country.

The entire family has been shaken to its core by Cristina's absence. Her 15 grandchildren do not understand why their grandmother is kept from them. One grandson goes into his abuela's closet and sniffs her clothes just so he can remember how she smells. Neither Procopio nor Cristina is sleeping well or eating properly and their physical and mental health is declining due to stress and sadness caused by the separation. To make matters more difficult, the end is not in sight.

Procopio has applied for a waiver. He has asked the government to grant his wife a visa to return to the States because he is suffering severe hardship by being separated from her.

The Military Method

Thousands of immigrants have served in every major American war since the American Revolution. In 2016, 511,000 foreign-born veterans were living in the United States, 3 percent of the members of the armed services. Gus Lee, the son of Chinese immigrants, said that in the Army, "It didn't matter what color you were or if you looked different or spoke with an accent or couldn't see straight. I was never before more equal as a human being than . . . in the Army."[6]

But Cristina's lawyer said the process can take between six and 18 months, and the likelihood of a waiver is only 50 percent. The process of assimilation for this family has been undone.

For many immigrant families, assimilation occurs at the same pace as it has for immigrants throughout American history. According to Audrey Singer, a senior fellow at the Urban Institute, "Immigrants are integrating on almost all measures. But the process takes place over people's lifetimes and across generations."[7] Many of today's immigrants simply have not lived in the United States long enough to fully integrate.

Assimilation is, however, visible in the children of immigrants. These youth grow up speaking English and are at home with American customs. Their income, job status, and home ownership are the same as everyone else's.

> ## Immigration is part of America's character and identity.

Despite the debate about immigration that ebbs and flows around her, Lady Liberty is not going anywhere. She still stands strong in the New York Harbor, torch aloft to guide immigrants through the Golden Door. The opening in that door may sometimes narrow, but it will never close completely. That is because if we lock the Golden Door, we close off a key part of our national identity. The United States is a nation of immigrants. For centuries, people have undergone great risks to find opportunity, freedom, and security, or to be with their loved ones on America's shores.

Today, the ancestors of those immigrants stand as evidence of one truth that has endured the test of time and should guide the nation's future: Today's immigrants become tomorrow's Americans.

VOCAB LAB

Write down what you think each word means. What root words can you find to help you? What does the context of the word tell you?

assimilate, **gross domestic product (GDP)**, and **visa**.

Compare your definitions with those of your friends or classmates. Did you all come up with the same meanings? Turn to the text and glossary if you need help.

KEY QUESTIONS

- **Is assimilation necessary for an immigrant's happiness in their new home?**

- **What should the goal of immigration policy be, keeping people out or finding ways of allowing them in?**

- **What do you think the future of immigration holds?**

MYTH-BUSTER INFOGRAPHIC

Humans have been designing infographics since Stone Age people painted on cave walls. An infographic is a visual representation of information. Infographics display data, map relationships, show trends, and provide insights into complex topics. Infographics rely on strong images and few words to make a complicated idea easier to understand. Work with a group of classmates or friends to design a series of infographics that bust common immigration myths.

- **Collect the data you need to dispel the myths.** Remember to evaluate your sources to make sure they are trustworthy.

- **What is the purpose of each piece of data you want to include on your infographic?** Knowing this will help you decide how to present that data. Here are some tips.

    1. To inform: Use large colorful fonts and icons to display statistics or facts.

    2. To compare: Use charts or pictograms to show similarities or differences.

    3. To show change across space and time: Use a line graph, timeline, or thematic map.

    4. To organize: Use a list, table, or flow chart.

- **Design your infographic.** Use a digital template (many websites offer them for free) or create your own from scratch. Create a natural flow of information on your graphic so the viewer can clearly understand the facts that bust the immigration myths.

This website has some examples of infographics created by professionals.

 freeyork infographics

- **Present your infographics to another group.**

To investigate more, present your infographics to the city council or school board. How does the response of an adult audience compare to that of your peers? If people disagree with your findings, what evidence do they provide to support their arguments? How does it feel to communicate publicly about a controversial topic?

CONSTRUCT AN
AMERICAN IDENTITY

In your journal, reflect on where a nation's identity comes from and how individuals with many different experiences and backgrounds can form a unified national character.

- **Create an identity chart for the United States.** Write "United States of America" in the middle of the paper and add words, phrases, and images that describe what it means to be an American.

- **Review the information in this book.** Consider the historical waves of immigration and the backlashes that tried to close the Golden Door. Ponder the statistics about the nation's changing demographics and the debates about immigration reform. Reflect on how immigration has enriched American culture. From this data, pull out more words, phrases, and statistics to illustrate how immigration is shaping America's identity.

- **Take stock of the chart.** What can you conclude about America's identity? Do some characteristics conflict with others? What might that mean about future conflict in the United States?

- **Create a collage of American identity in the twenty-first century.** A collage is a form of art made from assembling different materials to create a complete whole. A collage needs to have a unifying idea that links the various pieces together. What will your unifying idea be?

> **To investigate more,** survey people in your school and neighborhood, asking them, "What does it mean to be an American in the twenty-first century?" Identify common themes in their answers. Turn these common themes into words, phrases, or images and add them to your American identity chart.

GLOSSARY

abuela: the Spanish word for grandmother.

abusive: a person who is regularly cruel and insulting to others.

activist: a person who works for social or political change.

alien: a person who has come from another country.

Alien and Sedition Acts: a series of laws passed at the end of the nineteenth century designed to limit the public activities of people who sympathized with the French and criticized the government of U.S. President John Adams.

ally: to work together.

American dream: the idea that everyone who lives in the United States has an equal chance at success through hard work.

amnesty: a government pardon for a person who has committed a crime.

analogy: comparing two things for the purpose of explaining something.

anarchist: a person who does not believe that government and laws are necessary and wants to abolish them.

ancestor: a person from your family who lived before you.

anti-Semitic: prejudiced or hostile toward Jewish people.

apprehend: to arrest.

assembly line: a way of putting together products in a factory by passing materials from one machine or person to another to do the next step.

assimilate: to adapt to the customs and values of a new group or nation.

asylum: a protected status that governments can grant to immigrants fleeing a dangerous situation in their own country.

audit: to officially inspect a company's financial records.

background check: an investigation that looks up the criminal, commercial, and financial records of a person or organization.

backlash: a strong, negative reaction by a large group of people to a social or political event.

bail: a sum of money given to be temporarily released from jail. It is to guarantee that person's appearance in court.

balseros: the term used to refer to people who emigrate from Cuba on fragile, homemade rafts.

bankrupt: to be unable to repay debts.

barrio: an area in a Spanish-speaking town or city where many poor people live.

bias: the tendency to see or think of things a certain way based on previously held prejudices or beliefs.

Bill of Rights: the first 10 amendments to the U.S. Constitution that grant key protections to citizens, such as freedom of speech and religion.

bipartisan: the agreement or cooperation of two political parties that usually oppose each other's policies.

bioinformatics: the science of collecting and analyzing biological data such as genetic codes.

biometrics: the analysis of physical features such as fingerprints or voice patterns to verify someone's identity.

blight: a plant disease.

border: a line separating two political or geographical areas, especially countries.

Bracero Program: an agreement between the U.S. and Mexican governments that allowed Mexican laborers to come to the United States between 1942 and 1964.

brothel: a place where people pay to have sexual intercourse with prostitutes.

Buddhist: a person who follows the religion that teaches that suffering is part of life, but that you can get free of suffering through wisdom, virtue, and concentration.

burden: a heavy load.

bureaucracy: the system of nonelected officials who carry out many of the functions of government.

burkini: a swimming suit worn by some Muslim women that covers the entire body except the hands, feet, and face.

burqa: a long, loose garment that covers the entire body. It is worn in public by some Muslim women.

caucus: a conference of members of the legislature who belong to a particular political party or small group working on a particular issue.

census: an official count of the people living in a country.

cerebral palsy: a brain disorder that affects movement, muscle tone, and posture.

chain migration: the process by which green card holders can sponsor family members for permanent residency, who in turn can sponsor their family members.

chasm: a major separation between two sides.

citizen: a person who legally belongs to a country and has the rights and protection from that country.

citizenship oath: the pledge of loyalty a person must make before becoming a U.S. citizen.

Civil Rights Movement: the struggle by African Americans in the 1950s and 1960s to achieve equality to whites in employment, housing, education, and more.

colony: a group of people who form a settlement in a distant land, but remain under the control of the government of their native country.

compensate: to make up for something.

compromise: an agreement reached after both sides give up something they want.

conservative: a person who values traditional cultural or religious values and is reluctant to change them.

contagious: capable of being transferred from an infected person to another person by direct or indirect contact.

contract laborer: a worker (potentially from a foreign country) who is not an employee, but who is under contract to do work (sometimes only seasonally) for an employer.

controversial: an issue that causes disagreement.

corruption: the dishonest or illegal behavior of people in power.

coyote: a person who smuggles Latin Americans across the United States' border for a high fee.

criteria: the standard by which something is judged or measured.

culminate: to reach the final stage of something.

culture: the customs and beliefs of a group of people at a certain time in history.

customs agent: a government official who collects taxes on imports and exports.

Customs and Border Protection (CBP): the federal agency in charge of protecting United States' borders.

DACA (Deferred Action for Childhood Arrivals): an executive order signed by President Obama that allowed some people brought to the United States illegally as children to receive a renewable, two-year period of delayed deportation.

debate: a discussion of an issue in which people have opposing viewpoints.

defect: a flaw.

deluge: an overwhelming quantity of something.

democracy: a system of government where the people choose who will represent and govern them.

Democrat: a member of the Democratic Party, which typically believes in a broader reach of government.

Democratic-Republican: a political party of the early nineteenth century that wanted to restrict the power of the federal government and expand the power of the states.

demographics: the characteristics of a population, including age, gender, education, race, religion, and ethnicity.

deport: to expel an immigrant from a country, usually on the grounds of illegal status or for having committed a crime.

detain: to keep someone in official custody.

detention center: a place where people who entered the country illegally are kept in custody.

discriminate: to unfairly treat a person or group differently from others, usually because of their race, gender, or age.

displace: to force people from their homes, usually due to war, persecution, or natural disaster.

distortion: changing something out of its true, natural, or original state.

diversity: a range of different people or things.

diversity lottery: a pool of up to 50,000 immigrant visas randomly available every year to individuals who are from countries with low rates of immigration to the United States.

docket: a list of trial cases that will be heard in court.

earmark: to set aside funds for a particular purpose.

economy: the wealth and resources of an area or country.

embroil: to be deeply involved in a conflict.

emigrant: a person who leaves their own country in order to settle permanently in another one.

emigrate: to leave one's own country in order to settle permanently in another one.

endure: to put up with something difficult or painful without giving up.

ethnicity: the cultural identity of a person, including language, religion, nationality, customs, and ancestry.

ethnocentrism: judging another culture based on the values and standards of your own culture.

European Union: a political and economic union of 28 members, mostly in Europe.

exaggeration: a representation of something as larger, greater, better, or worse than it actually is.

executive power: the powers the president and cabinet members have to carry out and enforce the law.

expire: to stop being valid.

GLOSSARY

exploit: to take advantage of.

family preference: a type of visa for people who are more distantly related to a U.S. citizen or legal permanent resident than the visas allowed for immediate relatives.

family reunification: the immigration program through which immediate members of an immigrant's family are allowed to legally enter the United States.

Federalist: a political party in the late 1700s that favored a strong central government.

felon: a person who has committed a serious crime.

fiancé: someone engaged to be married to another person.

flash flood: a sudden flood due to heavy rain.

floodplain: the flat land next to a river that floods when the river overflows.

forge: to produce an imitation of something to deceive someone.

fragile state: a country whose government institutions are very weak and whose citizens suffer from poverty, violence, and political corruption.

fundamental: something that is of central importance.

genuine: authentic.

gerrymander: to manipulate the boundaries of a voting district to favor one political party.

green card: the documentation that shows you have been granted permanent residency in the United States.

gross domestic product (GDP): the total value of the goods and services produced in a country in one year.

guest worker: a person with temporary permission to work in another country.

heritage: the cultural traditions and history of a group of people.

human rights: the rights that belong to all people, such as freedom from torture, the right to live, and freedom from slavery.

human trafficker: a person who illegally transports people from one country to another.

hurdle: an obstacle that must be overcome in order to move forward.

hypocrisy: behaving in a way that contradicts what you claim to believe or feel.

ideal: a standard or belief that people strive to achieve.

identity: the characteristics that somebody recognizes as belonging uniquely to themselves.

illegal: a negative term often used to describe undocumented immigrants.

illiterate: unable to read and write.

immediate relative: for immigration law purposes, a spouse, minor child, or parent.

immigrant: a person who moves to a new country to settle there permanently.

immigrate: to move to a new country to settle there permanently.

ICE (Immigration and Customs Enforcement): an agency within the U.S. Department of Homeland Security that is responsible for enforcing federal immigration laws.

Immigration and Nationality Act: the 1965 law that abolished an earlier quota system based on national origin and established a new immigration policy based on reuniting immigrant families and attracting skilled labor to the United States.

immigration cap: the limit on the number of refugees accepted into the United States, set by the U.S. government.

immigration hold: when an undocumented immigrant who is already in jail is held past his scheduled release date to give ICE agents time to transfer him to a detention facility.

incentive: something that motivates or encourages someone to do something.

indefinitely: for an unlimited or unspecified period of time.

Industrial Revolution: a period of time during the eighteenth and nineteenth centuries when large cities and factories began to replace small towns and farming.

ineligible: not qualified.

influx: the arrival of large numbers of people.

initiate: to start a process.

international slave trade: the kidnapping and transportation of enslaved people from Africa to North and South America between the seventeenth and nineteenth centuries.

interracial: involving different races.

invest: to let someone else use your money with the possibility of getting more money back. What you invest in is called an investment.

ironic: when something happens in the opposite way of what is expected.

Jewish: Someone who believes in or identifies with Judaism; Judaism is a religion but has also at different times in history been described as a race, ethnicity, culture, and nation.

jurisdiction: the geographical region where a particular court or law enforcement official has the authority to administer and enforce the law.

Know-Nothing Party: an American political party prominent in the 1850s whose goal was to keep political power in the hands of native-born citizens.

kosher: food or drink that fits the requirements of Jewish dietary rules.

Latino: a person of Latin American origin or descent.

linguistic: having to do with the study of languages.

logical fallacy: an error in reasoning that makes an entire argument worthless.

malicious: intending to do harm.

mantle: an important role or responsibility that passes from one person to another.

Medicare: the federal health insurance program for the elderly.

metaphorical: using a word or phrase that normally means one thing to mean something else, such as "a sea of trouble."

migrant: a person who moves from one place to another, often with the change of seasons.

migrate: to move from one place to another, often with the change of seasons.

militia: a military force that engages in rebellion, usually in opposition to a country's regular army.

minority: a group of people that differs from the larger group in race, gender, language, religion, or in another way. Minorities are often discriminated against.

moral: relating to right and wrong behavior and character.

mortality: death on a large scale.

mosque: a Muslim place of worship.

Muslim: a person who follows the religion of Islam.

National Origin Act: an immigration law passed in 1924 that severely limited immigration based on country of origin. It discriminated against people from southern and eastern Europe and excluded Chinese immigrants.

nativist: favoring native-born inhabitants over foreigners.

naturalization: the process by which U.S. citizenship is granted to a foreign citizen or national after they fulfill the requirements established by Congress in the Immigration and Nationality Act (INA).

no-man's land: an area of unknown, unclaimed, or uninhabited land, often lying between two opposing groups.

open borders: a boundary between two countries that allows for free movement of people with few restrictions.

oppress: to use unjust or cruel authority and power to persecute someone.

order of removal: an order issued by an immigration judge that requires a person be deported.

overhaul: to examine something thoroughly in order to fix its flaws.

pastor: the minister in charge of a Christian church.

permanent residency: when a person is granted the legal right to permanently remain in a country of which they are not a citizen.

persecution: when people are treated cruelly or unfairly because of their membership in a social, racial, ethnic, or political group.

platform: the stated policies of a political party.

plight: an unfortunate, dangerous, or difficult situation

political: relating to a country's government.

political party: an organized group of people with similar political goals and opinions.

pollution: waste that harms the environment.

polygamist: a person who has more than one wife or husband at one time.

pope: the head of the Roman Catholic Church.

potato blight: a disease that destroys potato crops.

Powhatan: a member of a Native American people from Virginia.

prejudice: a preconceived opinion or judgment about someone that is not based on reason or actual experience.

priority: a thing that is regarded as more important than another.

proportion: a part or share of something.

prosecute: to carry out legal proceedings against someone accused of a crime.

Protestant: a member or follower of any of the Christian churches that are separate from the Roman Catholic Church.

psychological: pertaining to or affecting the mind.

quota: a limit on the number of people or objects.

race: a group of people of common ancestry who share certain physical characteristics such as skin color.

racism: negative opinions or treatment of people based on race and the notion that people of a different race are inferior because of their race.

radical: an extreme change from accepted or traditional practices.

raid: a rapid, surprise attack.

recruit: to enlist someone to do something.

reform: to improve something.

GLOSSARY

refugee: a person who has been forced to leave their country to avoid war, persecution, or natural disaster.

regulate: to control or supervise something.

Republican: a member of the Republican Party, which typically believes in less government and stronger states' rights.

residency: the fact of living in a place.

reunify: to bring separated families back together.

Revolutionary War: the war of independence fought between America and England between 1775 and 1783.

Roman Catholic: a member of a Christian church that has priests and bishops led by the pope.

sanctuary city: a city or town where the governing body has proclaimed it safe for undocumented immigrants to live, work, enroll in school, and otherwise live their lives without the fear of being arrested.

scandalous: disgracefully bad.

search warrant: a court order that allows police to search a property.

sedition: speech or behavior that encourages people to rebel against the government.

shun: to avoid, ignore, or reject someone.

slum: a heavily populated, run-down section of a city.

slur: an insult.

Social Security: a federal program that provides benefits to retired people and those who are unemployed or disabled.

socialism: the belief that people in society should be equal and workers should control the production of wealth in a country.

sociology: the study of human relationships and social problems.

sponsor: to give money and support.

statistics: numbers that show facts about a subject.

status adjustment: the process a person in the United States on a temporary visa uses to apply for lawful permanent residency status.

stereotype: an overly simple picture or prejudiced opinion of a person, group, or thing.

stopgap: a temporary way of dealing with a problem.

temporary nonimmigrant visa: a type of visa that allows a foreigner to stay in the United States for a short period of time, for example, to travel, work, or attend school.

tenement: a run-down, overcrowded apartment building.

terrain: the physical features of land.

terrorist: a person who uses unlawful violence and intimidation, especially against civilians, in pursuit of a political aim.

thesis statement: a short summary—often a single sentence—that condenses the main point of an essay, book, or theory.

torrent: a suddenly, violent outpouring of something.

trafficker: a person who trades in illegal goods.

trait: a characteristic.

transcript: the official record of a student's academic work in school.

unaccompanied minors: immigrant children traveling to the United States without an adult escort.

undocumented immigrants: people who have entered a country illegally.

unconstitutional: an act or policy that violates the U.S. Constitution, and is, therefore, illegal.

United Nations (UN): an international organization created to promote peace and cooperation among nations.

(USCIS) U.S. Citizenship and Immigration Service: the federal agency that oversees lawful immigration to the United States.

upsurge: a sudden increase in the strength of quantity of something.

vigilante: a person who takes the law into their own hands.

vigorous: done with lots of energy and effort.

visa: a document that allows the holder to enter, leave, or stay for a specific period of time in a country.

waive: when the government decides not to enforce a particular rule in an individual case.

Wampanoag: a member of the once-powerful Native American people who inhabited much of New England prior to the arrival of European settlers in the seventeenth century.

xenophobia: an intense or irrational dislike or fear of people from other countries.

zero-tolerance: the policy of giving the most severe punishment possible to all people who break a rule or law, regardless of their individual circumstances.

BOOKS

Bausam, Ann. *Denied, Detained, Deported: Stories from the Dark Side of American Immigration*. National Geographic, 2009.

Markham, Lauren. *The Far Away Brothers: Two Young Migrants and the Making of an American Life*. Crown, 2017.

Nazario, Sonia. *Enrique's Journey: The True Story of a Boy Determined to Reunite with His Mother*. Random House, 2013.

St. John, Warren. *Outcasts United: An American Town, a Refugee Team, and One Women's Quest to Make a Difference*. Spiegel & Grau, 2009.

MUSEUMS

Angel Island Immigration Station: aiisf.org

Ellis Island National Museum of Immigration: libertyellisfoundation.org/immigration-museum

Liberty Island: libertyellisfoundation.org/visiting-liberty-island

WEBSITES

Ellis Island Interactive Tour: teacher.scholastic.com/activities/immigration/tour/index.htm

Meet the New Americans: pbs.org/independentlens/newamericans/newamericans.html

Library of Congress Immigration in America: loc.gov/teachers/classroommaterials /presentationsandactivities/presentations/immigration/introduction2.html

QR CODE GLOSSARY

page 4: wbur.org/hereandnow/2016/04/18/immigrant-languages-new-york-city

page 6: buzzworthy.com/10-famous-immigrants-who-changed-america

page 15: embed.verite.co/timeline/?source=0Ark5K5szJsMSdD VpVVM2bHZ6UV9TRW5FajJXVmF3UkE&amp

page 16: youtube.com/watch?v=6_35a7sn6ds

page 17: hsp.org/education/primary-sources/letter-hannah-curtis-to-john-curtis-april-21-1847

page 20: smithsonianmag.com/history/pioneering-social-reformer-jacob-riis-revealed-how-other-half-lives-america-180951546

page 23: americanhistory.si.edu/exhibitions/bittersweet-harvest-bracero-program-1942-1964

page 25: nps.gov/trte/planyourvisit/maps.htm

page 26: dsl.richmond.edu/panorama/foreignborn/#decade=2010

page 32: youtube.com/watch?v=nKDgFCojiT8

RESOURCES

page 35: my.uscis.gov/prep/test/civics

page 39: youtube.com/watch?v=d9SPaEGJpLQ

page 46: pbs.org/pov/learning/video/it-would-be-worth-it-to-you

page 49: nytimes.com/interactive/2014/07/15/us/questions-about-the-border-kids.html

page 50: wola.org/analysis/children-fleeing-violence-central-america-face-dangers-mexico

page 53: humaneborders.info/app/map.asp

page 55: edu.gov.mb.ca/k12/cur/socstud/foundation_gr3/blms/3-2-3b.pdf

page 62: telegraph.co.uk/news/2017/01/29/protests-against-trumps-immigration-ban-pictures

page 67: welcomingamerica.org/programs/our-network

page 68: citylab.com/equity/2017/08/the-anti-sanctuary-cities-have-nearly-doubled/537516

page 68: cis.org/Map-Sanctuary-Cities-Counties-and-States

page 69: loc.gov/pictures/resource/pga.03047

page 78: folklife.si.edu/talkstory/2015/sounds-of-california-hearing-migration-through-music

page 79: loc.gov/teachers/classroommaterials/presentationsandactivities/
presentations/immigration/cuban_voc.html

page 81: loc.gov/teachers/classroommaterials/presentationsandactivities/
presentations/immigration/ckbk/index.html

page 94: splcenter.org/hate-map

page 108: freeyork.org/people/21-best-real-life-infographics

SOURCE NOTES

INTRODUCTION

1 Atwood, Kyle. "U.S. Hits Refugee Limit for 2017." CBS News. CBS. 12 July 2017.
Web. 1 May 2018. cbsnews.com/news/u-s-hits-refugee-limit-for-2017

2 Nicholson, Michael D., and CAP Immigration Team. "The Facts on Immigration
Today: 2017 Edition." Center for American Progress, americanprogress.org/issues/
immigration/reports/2017/04/20/430736/facts-immigration-today-2017-edition

3 Zeigler, Karen, and Steven Camarota. "U.S. Immigrant Population Hit Record 43.7 Million
in 2016." Center for Immigration Studies, Center for Immigration Studies, 16 Oct. 2017.
cis.org/Report/US-Immigrant-Population-Hit-Record-437-Million-2016

CHAPTER 1

1 DeSipio, Louis, and De la Garza, Rodolfo O. *US Immigration in the Twenty-First Century:
Making Americans, Remaking America.* Boulder, CO: Westview Press, 2015

2 DeSipio, Louis, and De la Garza, Rodolfo O. *US Immigration in the Twenty-First Century:
Making Americans, Remaking America.* Boulder, CO: Westview Press, 2015

CHAPTER 2

1 uscis.gov/working-united-states/permanent-workers

2 cnn.com/2018/04/27/us/mexico-migrant-caravan-diary/index.html

3 pewresearch.org/fact-tank/2018/01/29/where-displaced-syrians-have-resettled

4 cfr.org/backgrounder/how-does-us-refugee-system-wor

5 politifact.com/truth-o-meter/promises/trumpometer/promise/1397/build-wall-and-make-mexico-pay-it

6 Nicholson, Michael D., and CAP Immigration Team. "The Facts on Immigration Today: 2017 Edition." Center for American Progress, americanprogress.org/issues /immigration/reports/2017/04/20/430736/facts-immigration-today-2017-edition

7 factcheck.org/2018/04/the-stats-on-border-apprehensions

8 independent.co.uk/news/world/americas/trump-immigration-ice -workplace-raids-arrests-ohio-garden-center-a8385201.html

9 nytimes.com/2018/02/13/us/immigration-deportation-ice.html

10 usatoday.com/story/news/politics/2017/03/23/immigration-citizens-know-your-rights/99534722

11 freedomforimmigrants.org/detention-timeline

12 money.cnn.com/2017/04/13/news/economy/deportation-costs-undocumented-immigrant/index.html

CHAPTER 3

1 huffingtonpost.com/2014/06/17/unaccompanied-minors-central-america_n_5503908.html

2 bushcenter.org/publications/articles/2017/10/immigration-stories-tulip-nandu.html

3 migrationpolicy.org/article/south-american-immigrants-united-states-0

4 pewhispanic.org/2015/11/19/more-mexicans-leaving-than-coming-to-the-u-s

5 nbcnews.com/news/latino/nothing-us-here-deported-guatemalans-plan-return-u-s-n858231

6 migrationpolicy.org/article/middle-eastern-and-north-african-immigrants-united-states

7 pewresearch.org/fact-tank/2016/06/01/5-facts-about-the-global-somali-diaspora

8 time.com/5316584/world-refugee-day-visa-lottery-donald-trump-immigration

9 qz.com/1331069/the-death-rate-for-migrants-crossing-the-mediterranean-is-skyrocketing

CHAPTER 4

1 "Chapter 4: U.S. Public Has Mixed Views of Immigrants and Immigration." Pew Research Center's Hispanic Trends Project, 28 Sept. 2015. pewhispanic.org/2015/09/28 /chapter-4-u-s-public-has-mixed-views-of-immigrants-and-immigration

2 time.com/51518/obama-deportations-immigration

3 newsday.com/news/nation/donald-trump-speech-debates-and-campaign-quotes-1.11206532

4 theguardian.com/us-news/2015/dec/07/donald-trump-ban-all-muslims-entering-us-san-bernardino-shooting

5 newyorker.com/news/news-desk/the-mothers-being-deported-by-trump

6 time.com/5268572/jeff-sessions-illegal-border-separated

7 washingtonpost.com/local/immigration/nearly-250-migrant-children-still-separated-from-parents -aclu-report-says/2018/10/18/d3fc2fd0-d222-11e8-b2d2-f397227b43f0_story.html?utm_term=.209951b4a34a

8 Campbell, Alexia Fernández. "6 Immigrants Talk about the Anxiety of Living in Trump's America." *Vox*, Vox, 4 Aug. 2017. vox.com/policy-and-politics/2017/8/4/16069926/immigrants-trump-america.

9 Bornstein, David. "Immigrants Welcome Here." *The New York Times*, 19 Feb. 2014. opinionator.blogs.nytimes.com/2014/02/19/immigrants-welcome-here

RESOURCES

CHAPTER 5

1 huffingtonpost.com/entry/how-immigration-benefits-americans
-and-is-key-to-us_us_59b6db42e4b02bebae75f071
2 cbsnews.com/news/immigrants-impact-on-the-u-s-economy-in-7-charts
3 theatlantic.com/magazine/archive/2013/11/assimilation-nation/309518
4 politico.com/magazine/story/2016/09/trump-clinton-immigration-economy-unemployment-jobs-214216
5 vox.com/policy-and-politics/2018/7/30/17505406/trump-obama-race-politics-immigration
6 census.gov/newsroom/releases/archives/race/cb12-182.html
7 washingtonpost.com/news/business/wp/2018/05/22/i-am-not-a-racist-new-york-lawyer
-apologizes-for-rant-about-spanish-speakers-in-viral-video/?utm_term=.59472644ce7b
8 fb.org/issues/immigration-reform/agriculture-labor-reform/economic-impact-of-immigration

CHAPTER 6

1 obamawhitehouse.archives.gov/the-press-office/2011/03/28/remarks-president-univision-town-hall
2 unitedwedream.org/2011/05/obama-continues-to-deport-dreamers
3 time.com/daca-dream-act-jose-antonio-vargas-time-cover-revisited
4 youtube.com/watch?v=2ZbtFslcJUA
5 nytimes.com/2017/09/05/us/politics/trump-daca-dreamers-immigration.html
6 washingtonpost.com/powerpost/as-immigration-showdown-looms-in-senate-trump
-administration-is-doing-everything-in-our-power-to-stop-bipartisan-plan-official-says/2018/02/15
/e0cff9d0-1260-11e8-8ea1-c1d91fcec3fe_story.html?utm_term=.3e01bcbe75a6
7 vox.com/policy-and-politics/2018/7/30/17505406/trump-obama-race-politics-immigration

CHAPTER 7

1 cnn.com/2017/02/16/us/day-without-immigrants-vignettes/index.html
2 chicagotribune.com/business/ct-hospitality-needs-more-immigrants-report-0825-biz-20170824-story.html
3 economist.com/news/world-if/21724907-yes-it-would-be-disruptive
-potential-gains-are-so-vast-objectors-could-be-bribed
4 *Quartz* May 15, 2018
5 loc.gov/law/help/citizenship-birth-country/index.php
6 smithsonianmag.com/smithsonian-institution/how-unflinching-norman
-schwarzkopf-became-one-mans-guiding-light-180957425
7 bostonglobe.com/news/politics/2017/02/17/are-fighting-about-immigration
-assimilation/IDWgWjaqBrSRVIv1070qEL/story.html

INDEX

INDEX